GREED

The American Dream

Becomes a

Global Nightmare

KEN KOENEN, LLM

Writing Career Coach Press (a division of Writing Career Coach, 14665 Fike Rd., Riga, MI 49276) functions only as book publisher. As such, the ultimate design, content, editorial accuracy, and views expressed or implied in this work are those of the author.

ISBN-10 0983360723

ISBN-13 978-0-9833607-2-8

Cover Art by Zakr Studio. www.zakrstudio.com

Contents

Introduction

Preface

Oh, what a mess has been created in the real estate market. Foreclosures, short sales, job losses and no end in sight. All of this within a few short months after the peak of the real estate boom. What caused this sudden transformation that led to our current situation and economy?

The cause can be summed up in one word: GREED! Greed at all levels, although not with all people or groups.

When I first thought of writing this book two years ago, the original title of the book was going to be "Get Ready for the Next Real Estate Boom." Then I started experiencing through my clients the extent of the greed and corruption by a few at all levels within the industry as well as those wanting to profit from what everyone believed would be never ending growth of residential real estate. While not everyone was overtaken by greed, almost everyone was affected by what the minority was able to do.

It started with the deregulation of the banking and finance industries in 1982. Wall Street investment banking firms created new investment products which were known as Over the Counter (OTC) Derivatives. I use the term "products" loosely, because these were not really products in the sense of building a product that could be used and consumed by people.

One of the products in the beginning of the 2000's was mortgage backed securities. Billions in profits were made, and as they came more prevalent, the greed trickled down to the level of mortgage brokers, real estate agents and would be investors.

The collapse of the housing market in the United States had started a tsunami that affected millions of people around the globe.

In 1937, Napoleon Hill published his book, "Think and Grow Rich." In his book, he talked about the accumulation of wealth through thought, mastermind groups and self improvement. He also mentioned that wealth was one of those things that man craved, and they would try to obtain wealth through legitimate means of service to others, or through illegitimate means. He added that in the animal kingdom, because of the lack of thought capacity for animals, they would prey on other animals physically. However, because of the human's ability to think and reason, he could prey on other men financially. The men who succeeded in this arena, obtaining wealth at the expense of others, led to the calamity that the country and the world has faced in the past three years.

The residential real estate market was doing well. Prices were going up; interest rates were down, people were moving up and in many cases, keeping their old homes as investments or borrowing from the equity of their primary residence in order to invest in real estate.

As is normal when it comes to politics in America, the collapse of the economy brought with it the blame game. We will discuss these issues in more detail in this book. Many blame the Clinton administration and the changes made to the Community Reinvestment Act during his administration. The Community Reinvestment Act required FDIC banks to do more investing through loans to the local neighborhoods where they had branches in order to help moderate and low income households obtain housing.

Others blame the Bush administration, which wanted to make it easier for more people to own their own home, and encouraged lenders to provide programs to help the average person do so. Born was the sub-prime loan, the way to help those with a marginal credit history obtain financing, thus making financing easier to obtain. As we shall see, the sub-prime loans were aimed directly at those who could least afford a fluctuating interest rate, and had the least ability to understand the complexities of these loans.

On top of that, Wall Street was reeling from numerous scandals in the area of stocks and bonds. The accounting mismanagement of companies such as Enron, WorldCom and Tyco caused people who in the past had invested in the stock market to shy away from those types of investments. They needed a place to invest where they believed it would be safe, and still have a hedge against inflation.

The interest rate returns for Certificates of Deposit (CD's) rates were next to nothing, while real estate was appreciating at a slightly above normal pace, but nothing out of the ordinary, especially for California. So what happened?

Lenders then came up with stated income loans, where people with great credit could purchase a home (or a house for investment purposes) with no money down. Mortgage brokers and real estate agents began holding seminars on "How to Get Rich in Real Estate." They had no concern about the actual client, but only getting rich themselves through numerous commission checks.

No one, including the lenders and the ultimate investors of the cash that provided the funding, believed that the real estate market would ever go down. The belief was that "Real Estate values always go up in the America", especially in the Sun Belt states.

As shown in the following chapters, this unrealistic belief and the feeding of the frenzy created an artificial appreciation of real estate values throughout the United States. That was followed by the artificial depreciation caused by the rash of foreclosures and short sales by irrational lenders and investors.

It would affect the entire world. This book is intended to show in simple terms how this collapse happened, how everyone from the top to the bottom had a hand in it, and how government and lenders failed to recognize and address the problem before it became a disaster.

Fortunately, spring always follows winter, and it will again in the real estate market. After reviewing what caused the mess that we are currently in, I will discuss the reasons that this downturn will eventually lead to a rise in real estate prices and, if we are not careful, the next real estate boom.

I will also discuss ideas and warnings for investors of the future. While I fear that it will be many years away, and never at the level that was experienced from 2001 through 2006, real estate will still be a viable investment.

Chapter 1

What Is "The American Dream"?

The term was first used by James Truslow Adams in his book the Epic of America which was written in 1931. He states:

"The American Dream is "that dream of a land in which life should be better and richer and fuller for everyone, with opportunity for each according to ability or achievement. It is a difficult dream for the European upper classes to interpret adequately, and too many of us ourselves have grown weary and mistrustful of it. It is not a dream of motor cars and high wages merely, but a dream of social order in which each man and each woman shall be able to attain to the fullest stature of which they are innately capable, and be recognized by others for what they are, regardless of the fortuitous circumstances of birth or position."

Is that still the American Dream? Hardly! For many, the American Dream is merely surviving the day, emotionally, financially and every other way.

It all started out with such a noble goal. The idea of home ownership for more Americans so that they could appreciate the security of owning rather than renting a home was indeed noble. The loan programs would provide a chance for those who had previously made mistakes or had circumstances in their lives that caused problems with their credit that prevented them from reaching for the American Dream. It was believed that owning your own home would make a homeowner a better person who could better take care of his family.

Who knew that what was to come would turn the "American Dream" into the American Nightmare, and ultimately, the Global Nightmare!

Unfortunately, the structure that was created was based solely on the notion that the real estate market would appreciate on a never ending basis. Loan programs, mortgage backed securities, home purchaser and those who purchased shares of the mortgage backed securities all shared in that belief.

Of course, as we all know, what goes up must come down. In order to see how the mess was created, one must start in the past.

How Real Estate Financing Worked in The Past

I have always believed that in order to understand where you are, one must remember the path that he or she took to get there in the first place. The desire to own land dates back many centuries. The ability to and method of obtaining and financing the purchase of real estate has evolved over the years.

As far back as the beginning of human existence, there has been a desire to possess things. Today, everything is owned or controlled by some other person, company or government. Even when the

11

things that could be possessed were plentiful, man has always desired to own the nicer "thing" that was owned or controlled by someone else.

For Sale

Even in prehistoric times, I would believe that if someone had a nicer cave, someone else would want it for himself. The illustration above possibly reflects the first recorded history of man using trickery and deception in obtaining real estate. Prior to that, it was accomplished through the concept of "Survival of the Fittest." If someone had something you wanted, and he was weaker than you, he just came and took it by force. If two people had equal strength, the one who wanted something more would either have to negotiate for it by trading something of value or using trickery to obtain it.

In medieval times, the land was controlled by the lords, and the serfs worked the land and were allowed to live there as long as they were producing for the lords. Later, the lords would sell the land to the serfs using land sales contracts and, ultimately, mortgages. The difference was that title never passed to the buyer until the last payment was made. A buyer could have made all of the promised payments, except for the last one, and have the contract foreclosed, and he would lose all of the past payments that had been made.

The government and courts of the time stepped in, believing this to be unfair, and created a "right of redemption", which would allow the buyer an opportunity to make up for those final payments and regain the final ownership of the property.

In America's "Old West", especially after gold was discovered in California, the land belonged to no one other than the territory and the government. Still encouraging growth and the exploitation of the vast natural resources available in the West, settlors could go to California, find a location that appeared to have some gold reserves, and stake a claim for that land.

Unfortunately, where there is land and wealth available, greed, force and trickery are not far behind. Once the settlor had staked his claim and started a mining operation, gangs of bandits (claim jumpers) would try to overrun the settlor, either by scaring him off or murdering him. The more sophisticated "bandits" would get the settlor to unwittingly sign over his claim to them. Many of the settlors were basically illiterate, and had no idea what they were signing.

Prior to the Great Recession that occurred after the Stock Market Crash of 1929, mortgage loans were, for the most part, short term (5 year) interest only loans. When the 5 years were over, you simply refinanced at the current interest rates. When the stock market crashed, the money supply dried up, there was no money to loan and the mortgage holders began foreclosing when the homeowners could not refinance or pay off the loan.

The Glass-Steagall Act, also referred to as the Banking Act of 1933, placed a number of restrictions

13

on banks, most of which were repealed through the process of deregulation. To fully understand deregulation, it's helpful to first understand why regulatory laws were enacted.

Glass-Steagall Act - The 1929 stock market crash and the Glass-Steagall Act were essentially the bookends to the Great Depression. From 1900 to 1929 the Bank of the United States underwrote corporate stocks, artificially inflating the market. This culminated in the crash, when all banks in the United States closed for four days, with over 4,000 never reopening. This led to a run on the banks, which spawned the Great Depression. The Glass-Steagall Act was passed in direct response to the Great Depression and helped to stabilize and rebuild the nation's economy. It expanded the regulatory powers of the Federal Reserve, prohibited banks from trading in corporate securities and created the Federal Deposit Insurance Corporation (FDIC).

After struggling through the Depression, the Federal Housing Administration (FHA) was formed, and the 30-year, fixed rate loan was introduced. Now there was no need to refinance every 5 years. Things worked very simply.

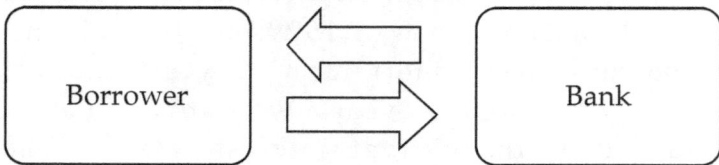

If you decided to purchase a home, you simply went to the bank where you have had relationships over the years, and applied for a loan. You met with the bank manager who took the application. After reviewing your qualifications, your application would go in front of the "loan committee", who would either approve or reject your loan. There were no FICO scores, no credit reporting agencies, and no formulas. The committee made the decision based on your history with the bank and your ability to handle the payments.

Congratulations ... your loan was approved, and you are now a homeowner. Over the next 30 years, you made your monthly payments, and sometimes more than the minimum, until the day you paid off your mortgage. On that day, you would invite your friends, the banker, anyone who would come over, and you would have a big party where you burned the mortgage to celebrate.

Your home was your castle, and you were free of debt.

How It All Changed

Many have pointed to the "Community Reinvestment Act of 1977" as the birth of free and easy credit. The Community Reinvestment Act is intended to encourage depository institutions to help meet the credit needs of the communities in which they operate, including low- and moderate-income neighborhoods, consistent with safe and sound banking operations. It was enacted by the Congress in 1977 (12 U.S.C. 2901) and is implemented by Regulations 12 CFR parts 25, 228, 345, and 563e. But there have been a number of deregulatory steps that have led to where we are today.

Beginnings of Deregulation - Until the 1970s banking was governed primarily by state laws, and banks could do business only in their home states. A Nebraska bank solicited customers from Minnesota but charged them Nebraska's higher interest rate. Minnesota's Marquette Bank[1] filed a lawsuit to stop this practice, and the case went to the Supreme Court. In its "Marquette Decision," the Court ruled that banks could charge the interest rates allowed in the state of the issuing bank rather than the amount allowed in the states where the credit card holder was residing. In essence, the banks were allowed to export their state's allowable interest rates into other states. This decision prompted banks to establish headquarters in states that would allow them to charge the highest interest rates, which caused the tax base of those states grow substantially. To stay competitive, other states raised caps on the interest rates banks could charge. This effectively led to the deregulation of state interest laws, also known as usury law. There are so many exceptions to the usury laws in California now that it leaks like a sieve.

Depository Institutions Deregulation and Monetary Control Act of 1980 -The Depository Institutions Deregulation and Monetary Control Act of 1980 (DIDMCA) abolished state caps on interest rates that could be charged for primary mortgages, giving banks the incentive to approve mortgages for people with problematic credit histories. Banks made more money by charging higher rates to riskier customers, and a broader range of people were able to purchase homes. These loans were for the most part fixed rate mortgages and were freely assumable by a subsequent

---

[1] Marquette Nat. Bank v. First of Omaha Svc. Corp., 439 U.S. 299 (1978)

purchaser without approval from the lender, either by the terms of the loan or because of state law.

For example, the California Supreme Court stated that in order to enforce a due on sale clause, a lender must demonstrate that enforcement is reasonably necessary to protect against impairment to its security or the risk of default.[2] This was not an easy an easy threshold of proof to reach, and most lenders would not make the effort to do so.

In the late 1970's and early 1980's, the country suffered from runaway inflation. Prices were increasing daily for all commodities, including housing. In an attempt to control inflation, the government repeatedly raised the prime interest rate, which caused the interest rate for home mortgages to exceed 14%-18% in order to purchase a home. The prime rate charged by banks to their best customers jumped to over 20%! Homeownership and real estate values skyrocketed in spite of these exorbitant interest rates. How did this happen?

Most of the loans were done with "Creative Financing". Most of the existing loans on properties being sold were in the 6%-7% range. Buyers would make a 10%-20% down payment, "take subject to" or informally assume the seller's loan, and either obtain a second mortgage from an institutional lender, or have the seller carry a second mortgage. Another method was the All-Inclusive Deed of Trust, or the "Wrap-Around Mortgage."

Unfortunately, the banks and savings and loans suffered, because they had outstanding loans for which they were receiving 6%-7% interest; while at

---

[2] Wellenkamp v. Bank of America, 21 Cal.3d 943 (1978)

the same time, they were paying close to 15% in borrow money from the Federal Government.

All of that changed in 1982 when the United States Supreme Court issued a new ruling on the subject of due on sale clauses, as they applied to the Savings and Loan industry. In its decision, the Court stated that "we hold that the Board's due-on-sale regulation bars application of the Wellenkamp rule to federal savings and loan associations"[3] and thereby overturned the appeals court that had relied on the Wellenkamp decision in its ruling. The due on sale clause was about to meet its doom.

Garn-St. Germain Depository Institutions Act of 1982 – This was known as "An Act to revitalize the housing industry by strengthening the financial stability of home mortgage lending institutions and ensuring the availability of home mortgage loans." There are a number of parts of this act, one of which prohibited the states to enforce any laws that barred a Due on Sale clause in the mortgage contracts or deeds of trust for Federal lending institutions. The banks responded by enforcing their due on sale clause in their promissory notes and deeds of trust, requiring that the loan be paid in full upon the sale of the property. If a seller attempted to sell the property using a second or wrap around mortgage, the lender could accelerate the loan and demand full payment of the mortgage. Failure to pay off the loan would result in a possible foreclosure.

In order to continue to stimulate the real estate market and provide a method by which both the buyers and the lenders could be spared from the pain

_____

[3] Fidelity Federal Savings and Loan Assn. v. De La Cuesta, 458 U.S. 141 (1982)

18

of fluctuating interest rates, the adjustable loan was developed. These adjustable loans were designed to share the risk and reward of fluctuating interest rates. They were set to an "Index" that could rise or fall, depending on the economy. If the Index rate went up, the interest rate on the loan would increase. If the Index rate dropped, the interest on the loan, and thus the monthly payment, would decrease.

Title VIII of the Garn – St. Germain act was the Alternative Mortgage Transactions Parity Act of 1982 - Before the Alternative Mortgage Transactions Parity Act of 1982 (AMTPA), all mortgages were fixed-rate amortizing loans. Interest rates were still incredibly high, and most people could not qualify for new loans based on these higher rates. This legislation opened the doors to nontraditional mortgages, thus paving the way for adjustable rates, balloon payments, interest-only loans, and optional adjustable rates. Many of these loans allowed borrowers to make payments at a substantially lower monthly payment and interest rate during the first few years of the loan, with the idea that the borrowers' incomes would go up as the years went by. Lenders would use those lower starting payments when the borrowers were qualifying for the loans.

In the mid to late 1980's, the real estate market was going through double digit appreciation. The lenders, led by World Savings, developed the "Stated Income" loan application. If the borrower was unable to verify his income, whether because they were self-employed or receiving income that could not be completely verified (child support, alimony, etc.), they could simply state the income without providing verification. The key to the success of these loans

19

was that the lender would require a 20% down payment in order to approve the loan. In other words, the lender would only provide an 80% loan to value against the property. If values dropped (as they did in 1989-1992), the lenders had a 20% cushion.

Although there were some serious problems with foreclosures during that time frame, they generally affected the higher priced property. Those properties dropped by as much as 50% in value, while the low to moderate priced homes only fell by 10%-15%. This downturn, which was one of the first times when California real estate values significantly fell, was fairly short lived, lasting about one year, and leveling off for another 2 years or so. Of course the double digit increases in values that preceded the downturn was equally short.

Riegle-Neal Interstate Banking and Branching Efficiency Act of 1994 - The Riegle-Neal Interstate Banking and Branching Efficiency Act of 1994 (IBBEA) swept away all state barriers to interstate banking. It allowed financial institutions to locate branches in other states and to purchase or merge with banks headquartered in other states. Bank of America, once a California bank, crossed the country with branches everywhere.

Gramm-Leach-Bliley Act - The Gramm-Leach-Bliley Act (GLBA), also referred to as the Financial Services Modernization Act of 1999, repealed part of Glass-Steagall, tearing down the walls between banking, insurance and investments. Companies could now merge, partner and operate freely within each other's industries. State Farm Insurance now had State Farm Bank. Citicorp now had Citicorp Insurance

Company. Even H&R Block got into the act, acquiring its own bank.

The act also made it easier for the financial industry to group mortgage and other portfolios, selling them as investments. One of the pioneers of the "securitization" of mortgages was Lewis Ranieri, who was head of the mortgage desk at Solomon Brothers, and investment bank, in the 1980's. He now understands how much harm has been caused by the sub-prime loans, and is now trying to make amends by helping people remain in their homes.

The real estate market remained relatively steady from 1992 to 1995 with appreciation rates that brought many homes back to their 1989 levels. In 1995, the internet really began taking hold with thousands of new high tech jobs, low interest rates, prosperity, and over-night 28 year old millionaires were created when new start up internet companies went public.

This was also the time when online stock brokers, such as E-Trade became popular. It did not take much to become a "Day-Trader," and many people would sit at home all day buying and selling stock. This helped drive the stock market from 4,000 in 1994 to almost 12,000 in 2000, during the Clinton administration.

The computer age meant that more transactions could take place in the same amount of time, and volume became the goal. No one was interested in building long term, sustainable businesses anymore. The idea of starting a Ford Motor Company, an IBM, or a Microsoft was passé. The notion of building a company for the long term and generating a good, consistent income no longer existed. Everyone wanted instant gratification and instant wealth.

Everyone wanted to jump onto the Dot-Com wagon and come up with a website that would lead them to millions of dollars in a couple of years. Build it up, spend hundreds of thousands to get it known, and then take it public for millions of dollars. People tried everything, from dry clean pick up service to grocery delivery. I got involved with a company called ZipRealty.com, which advertised itself to be the first online real estate company, which it was. Unfortunately, they got into the game a little late, and by the time they were in a position to go public, the bloom was off the rose of the Dot Com companies.

Companies that had existed for years, making a fair profit and paying dividends to their investors, were now more intent on getting the stock prices to go up rather than to make a solid, sustainable business. The accountants "cooked the books" to make the income statement and balance sheets to look better than they really were. The executives took hefty bonuses and were able to sell their stock when it was high. The regular stock holders, and sometimes employees, were swindled by the officers and board of directors of companies. We already mentioned Enron, but around the same time there was accounting fraud with WorldCom, Global Crossing and Tyco.

They manipulated the balance sheets to show profitability, in order to draw in more investors, and the leaders of those companies received massive bonuses. Eventually, the house of cards collapsed and the businesses ceased to exist. The United States Government, who was supposed to regulate corporations, and the accounting firms, who were charged with making sure that the financials were accurately stated, failed miserably in their jobs at the expense of millions of investors and employees.

The "American Dream" had become, "Make a million fast." Unfortunately, a few additional words were soon added to that "Dream." The sentence was changed to, "Make a million fast, at any cost."

The age of technology and being able to process information at an alarming pace, the greed of people to become instant millionaires, along with the lack of morality to do so in a manner that served others instead of at the expense of others, created the Bermuda Triangle.

It was the making of the perfect storm to lead the country and the world into the greatest recession since the Great Depression.

Chapter 2

The Mortgage Mess - The Rise

1. Mortgage Backed Securities

As the demand for homes increase, so did the demand for money. Banks started leveraging their depositors' money in order to finance more new loans. New loan products were introduced, such as interest only payments and negative amortization, where the principle balance would actually increase each month because the payments made by the borrower was less than the interest being charged.

There was a cushion for the lenders when down payments were less than 20%, known as Private Mortgage Insurance, or PMI. With PMI, the borrower could make a down payment of 5-10% and obtain a 90-95% loan with the difference between the 80% loan to value and the amount of the loan guaranteed by the mortgage insurer.

The PMI insurer provided a second set of eyes to review the strength of the borrower to make sure he had the ability to make the payments. There was an insurance premium that was added to every payment in order to cover possible losses from the insured pool of homeowners. If the real estate value of the property went up to where there was a 75% or less loan to value, the PMI could be terminated.

The banks saw the amount of money that was being paid in premiums to the PMI companies, and decided that those funds should go into their pockets. They came up with the 80-10-10 loan. The buyer would put 10% down, and get an 80% first loan and a 10% second loan at a higher interest rate. The payments on the two loans combined was usually less than the payments would be on a 90% loan with PMI, and the bank received the additional interest income, although it had lower protection than with PMI.

Those loans became so successful, that the lenders took the next natural step of providing 80-15-5 loans and eventually 80-20 loans, where the first loan was 80% of the purchase price and the second was a Home Equity Line of Credit (HELOC) for the remainder of the purchase price. The banks were getting higher interest rates on the second mortgages, and the buyers were risking only some closing costs and their credit records if they failed to pay.

Then, a few lenders actually came up with programs where the borrower could borrow up to 125% of the value of the property they were purchasing. It was usually claimed that the additional amount was being used for refurbishing the property, but in reality many times the buyers received a substantial check at close of escrow instead of paying any down payment or closing costs.

Prices started going up because of all of the new buyers coming along with these programs. The problem was that the second set of eyes was not there to review the information that was being provided.

But where was all of this money coming from? The answer is Residential Mortgage Backed Securities (RMBS).

Have you ever been to a baseball game, and as you are entering the stadium, someone is there selling a program, and informing everyone walking by that "You can't tell the players without a program." Well, that is pretty much what you will need to do to follow the flow of the RMBS system.

The chart on the following page demonstrates the complexities of the system that was developed, and why the lenders who were generating the loans did not care about the quality of the mortgages. The loans were being packaged and sold to investors as Residential Mortgage Backed Securities. Look at the flow chart following the next few paragraphs, to see how it worked:

1.   The Borrower would go to the Lender or a Mortgage Broker who would arrange for a loan with a Lender.
2.   When the Lender had enough loans, it would package those loans into a "Special Purpose Entity" (SPE) Trust to hold the mortgages.
3.   They would then have these Trusts rated by a Bond Underwriter which would package them as securities for sale.
4.   Bond insurance would be obtained, and rating companies, such as Moody's or Standard and Poor's, provided an AAA rating for the securities.
5.   The Bonds would then be sold to institutional investors which would also sell them to individual investors.

26

6.   The proceeds from the sale of the Bonds would go back to the Trustee of the SPE Trust and then back to the original Lender. Now the Lender had fresh money to start the process again.

7.   Often times, the Lender would retain control of the servicing of the loans, for a fee, which is why many people would think that the loan was owned by Countrywide, for example, when in reality it had been packaged into a trust whose shares were owned by thousands of individuals and entities.

Since the lenders had no vested interest in

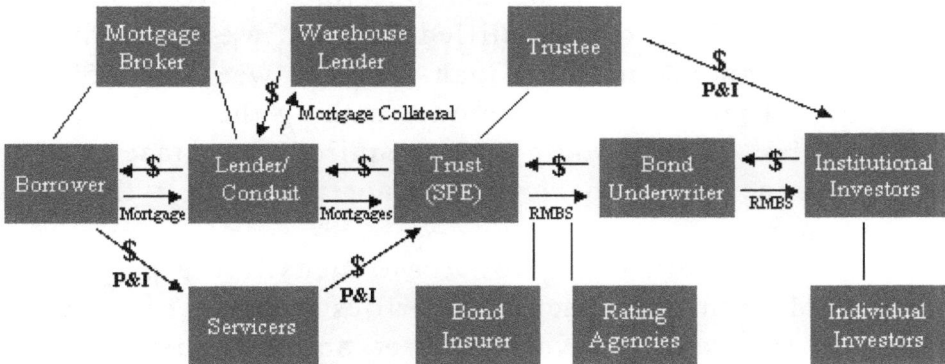

whether or not the mortgages went bad, they loosened up the lending criteria and came up with loans that made a mortgage available to almost anyone who could breathe or lie about it. The goal was to make money processing the loan, make money selling the loan and make money servicing the loan.

The computer systems for the lenders, with Countrywide leading the pack, became so sophisticated that they could determine in October how many mortgages that they would have available in December to sell, have them pre-packaged and sold with a guarantee that at least 50% of the loans would have pre-payment penalty clauses. They would be able to sell these packages at 102% of the face value of the loan amounts. I will explain why they were able to get this kind of return a little later in this chapter.

You remember the chart in the first chapter showing the link between the borrower and the lender bank in the past. The lender was on the hook if the borrower did not repay the loan. That simple scenario changed to the chart shown above.

Now take this chart and add two more layers; one for "B" paper loans and one for "C" paper loans. In 1992, if you only qualified for what was defined as a "C" paper loan, your loan to value was only 65%-70%. That is because the ones making the loans were at risk, and would be required to face the consequences if the loan was not repaid in a timely manner.

The ability to throw these loans into a package called "mortgage backed securities", shares of which were then sold to investors based on the Credit Rating Agencies evaluation, created an atmosphere where those making the loans were able to totally disregard any issues such as repayment.

What was once a simple process was now a tangled web of thousands of businesses and individuals with only one goal. That was to make money at any cost, even if that included taking advantage of potential buyers.

2. The Birth of Sub-Prime Loans

Money was cheap because interest rates were at an all time low. Lenders were making their money, not by collecting the interest over many years, but by making loans, packaging millions of dollars of these loans and then selling them to the government (FHA, Fannie Mae, etc.) and to private investors. From the funds of the sale of these loans, the lender would make a profit and obtain new funds with which to make more loans.

No one could get enough business with the "normal" loan products that were available, so they came out with new programs in order to increase their flow.

"Low Doc", "No Doc" and "Stated Income" loan programs came into being. These types of loans, they have been around for many years, but normally required significant down payments and some realistic basis that the individual borrowing the money was actually making the money claimed. For example, a "Stated Income" loan in 1989 required a 20% down payment. While there was some abuse at the time with these loans, for the most part they were helpful and protected the lender from loss due to abuse. They were a valuable tool in the mortgage business for legitimate buyers.

The lenders now started offering stated income loans to buyers with no money down based upon the amount of income the borrower claimed to make and his credit, or FICO, score.

Automation also helped to increase the number of new applications that could be processed. The lenders were no longer closely reviewing the credit

29

reports. Instead, they would use the "Middle" FICO score. There were 3 major credit reporting companies; Experian, Equifax and Trans Union. They each assigned a score to the credit report, and although they were called by different names, they were referred to as the FICO scores. Lenders would throw out the high and the low scores, and base their decision on the middle score.

The new loan programs that came out allowed for purchases with no down payment. Anyone could get a zero down, stated income loan if their FICO scores were high enough. Eventually, the lenders ran out of buyers with good FICO scores, and started lowering the scores needed for a purchase. After all, prices would always go up, so if a few didn't pay, the investor could simply foreclose.

Even that was not good enough to satisfy the greed factor, so the criteria for qualifications (meaning FICO score) was relaxed even more to the point where someone with a low 500 FICO score could get 100% financing on the purchase of a home. If you could not qualify to purchase a home, your credit must have really been horrible.

While many mortgage professionals understood the meaning of "stated incomes", others used it to mean that they could write in anything they wanted in order to get a loan approved. I had one client come to me about a year after she had purchased a home because she realized that the loan that she had was a negative amortized loan, and her balance was going up every month. She brought in the credit application that she had signed for the mortgage broker, and it showed that she made $6300 per month. When I looked at the application that had been submitted to the lender, it included another $6,000 per month income. The broker had added that, in addition to her regular job, she did wedding planning in the evenings and weekends, and that was the source of her other income.

These individuals were ignorant, poorly trained, dishonestly trained or just plain dishonest!

The other issue that came up was the various adjustable rate programs that we discussed earlier. Interest only, negative amortization, 2 year fixed with large adjustments at the end of the two years. The mortgage brokers told buyers that the market would continue to go up forever and that when the adjustment came, they would simply refinance the loan to a new program and new rate. As we shall see, that came to an end when credit tightened.

3. An Influx of Real Estate Agents –

Where there is money to be made, people will flock to the source. In this case, thousands of people became real estate agents and mortgage brokers. Some of these people had no idea what they were doing, and did not go to work for brokers who would properly train them.

A brief look at history will explain the scenario. The number of real estate licensees increased steadily from 1971, with a total of about 160,000, to about 425,000 in 1980. During the same period, the membership numbers in the California Association of Realtors (CAR) grew from less than 60,000 to 148,350. During that time period, the real estate values increased by an average of 27% per year.

In 1980, we were hit with double digit inflation along with a nagging recession. Real estate sales slowed down, and the number of real estate agent

31

plummeted. Between 1980 and 1983, the number of licensees dropped to about 320,000, while the number of CAR members dropped by almost 44,000 to 102,600. During that time period, the market averaged only 5% appreciation per year.

Between 1985 and 1989 the market again increased at a rate of 16% per year. Can you guess what happened? The number of licensees, after dropping to about 290,000 mushroomed back to 370,000 in 1990. The number of CAR members went back up to 146,000.

In 1989, the real estate market slowed down, with the median price of homes falling for the first time in history. The reasons for that decline were completely different from today's problems, as they were purely economic. There had been a stock market collapse, a major earthquake in the Los Angeles area, and the collapse of the Soviet Union significantly hurt the aerospace and defense industries in California. For the first time, more people left the state than came into the state.

Between 1989 and 1996, the median priced home in California dropped an average of 2% per year. During that same time period, the number of licensed real estate agents fell to a total of approximately 300,000, while membership at CAR dropped to 90,000 – the lowest since 1976!

From 1997 to 2006, the number of licensed real estate agents shot up to about 524,000, and the number of CAR members more than doubled to about 210,000 members. Not surprisingly, the median price of a home in California increased at an average rate of 21% per year.

Why is there such a disparity between licensed real estate agents and the CAR membership? CAR

members belong to one of the local board of Realtors®
and their primary function is to act as an agent to help
people buy or sell real estate. Mortgage brokers and
agents do not normally belong to CAR.

Now that we have seen all of these statistics,
what does that have to do with what happened in the
real estate market? There are a number of reasons
that these new agents and mortgage brokers caused the
artificial appreciation in real estate.

Real estate is a profession that requires skill,
training and mentoring by other experienced
professionals. The problem that occurred, at least in
California, was that new licensees could immediately
become a real estate Broker by 1) having a 4 year
college degree, and 2) passing the California Real
Estate Broker's exam (not a very difficult test). Once
they did that, they could open an office, hire real
estate sales agents, and "manage" those agents even
though they had never sold or listed a house for sale
in their lives.

Now compare that to what it takes to become an
appraiser in California. One must to do a little more
than just pass a test. As shown on the California
Office of Real Estate Appraiser Website, there are
steps that must be taken:

Levels of Licensure

There are four levels of real estate appraiser
licensing. They are:
- AT - Trainee License
- AL - Residential License
- AR - Certified Residential License
- AG - Certified General License

33

While I won't go into the details of what is involved in obtaining each level of licensing, suffice it to say that there are hundreds of hours of education and supervision by other experience appraisers involved in moving from one level of license to the next.

Individuals seeking a contractor's license in California also must have a certain amount of experience while working under another contractor, as well as completing a written examination.

No such "experience" requirement exists in California for a real estate Broker. Why is that a big deal? The answer to that is very simple ... they did not know what they were doing, and were susceptible to the influence of others. Some mortgage brokers were hiring people who had not even taken the real estate exam or taken a real estate course, and had those individuals handling functions that required a real estate license. The brokers called them "Loan Processors", but those individuals did everything that a licensed mortgage agent would do, and received payment in the form of commissions.

Another area that has always created a conflict, in my mind, is that of "dual agency." I will get a lot of arguments from real estate agents regarding dual agency, but I believe that in the form that it now exists, it should be banned. What is dual agency? That is a situation where one agent (or agency) represents both the buyer and the seller. How can you be looking out for the best interest of both parties? That would be like me, as an attorney, representing both the plaintiff and the defendant in an adversarial proceeding. It cannot be done. Furthermore, when the transaction is over (if not before) one or both of the clients is thinking that you are working harder for the other guy.

Thousands of real estate agents were acting with no real training or supervision, or the training that they did receive was how to manipulate the system with the loan products that were available. Their "Broker of Record" for the companies the agents worked for were just using their licenses to make a few extra dollars. They had no experience in running a real estate or mortgage business, and never provided any substantive training or supervision of their agents.

Other Brokerages opened in the San Francisco Bay area, as well as others, which had almost 300 licensees under the corporate umbrella, from all corners of the state. There was no way that the brokers could possibly have managed, supervised or trained each of them, nor did they have a network of managers in different areas to manage the agents. They were all on their own, and in many cases consistently defrauded their clients and lenders, just to make a buck. They learned the tricks from others, and their primary goal was to get rich quick at any cost. I will explain how that was able to happen in the next chapter.

4.   Lender Representatives Were Greedy, Too.

Lenders representatives, including those from some of the big name banks, actually coached mortgage brokers and agents on how to prepare the loan package in order to get the loans through the system and past the underwriter. The standard line was "you know what to do to get it through!" Some of the things that they were teaching were outright loan fraud.

Even in-house lenders with organizations like Countrywide Home Loans were working with real estate agents to put together fraudulent transactions. I had a case in which a couple was on the verge of foreclosure, and could not make their payments. A real estate agent, working with an in-house loan agent from Countrywide concocted a scheme whereby a man with limited skills in English, and practically no knowledge of the real estate business, was convinced to purchase a house, which he would then rent back to the owner.

The owner received the proceeds from the sale and the lender and the real estate agent received their commissions. However, the previous owners refused to move out, and the unsuspecting "buyer" attempted to have them evicted. Unfortunately, the transaction violated the Home Equity Sales Act, which was designed to protect those in foreclosure from unscrupulous foreclosure consultants and buyers. The original owners remained in the property for another 6-7 months without making any additional payments, until Countrywide foreclosed.

Now, remember, this was at a time when the market was still booming and prices were continuing to increase. The net result was that the unsuspecting "buyer" lost money and had his credit irreparably harmed.

5. Yield Spreads

I mentioned earlier that I would tell you why companies such as Countrywide could guarantee that half the loans would have prepayment penalties, which enabled them to sell the loans for more than face value. It was through "yield spreads.

Mortgage brokers not only received a commission for putting a loan together, but could also receive what was known as a "yield spread". What is a yield spread? Well, if you can get the borrower to accept a certain program that benefited the lender, an additional fee would be paid to broker! Often, these fees were as much as 3% of the loan amount, on top of the fees the broker was already collecting. What would trigger these fees?

Loans with higher interest rates after the start rate. Adjustable loans instead of fixed loans. Prepayment penalties that would lock in a borrower so they could not refinance for a certain period of time without paying the penalty, even if the rates went down.

Because many of the people did not understand the confusing papers that they were signing, they had no idea that they were committing themselves to such high interest rates and prepayment penalties. Before long, these loans started adjusting at a time when the borrowers were no longer able to refinance.

Mortgage brokers were rewarded by the lenders with bonuses of as much as 3% more than they would normally receive for a loan transaction.

Didn't these need to be disclosed to the borrower? Of course, but it was just another piece of paper in the midst of dozens, which in many cases were never explained to or read by the Borrowers.

6. Real Estate Agents Become Mortgage Brokers, Too.

Then things got really fun! Real estate agents began acting as mortgage brokers, as well as representing buyers and sellers in real estate transactions. This new ability created scenarios that really tested the ethics of many real estate agents. A real estate agent has a fiduciary duty to his client (principal), and the laws of agency control their activities.

What could possibly happen when Real Estate agents started doing loans as well as represent buyers and sellers? A real estate agent representing a seller of property could end up representing 5 transactions! Think about it. An agent represents the seller, and meets a buyer at an open house. He gets the buyer to make an offer, using the agent's services as a real estate agent and as a mortgage broker. He is going to represent the seller in the sale of his house, as well as when purchasing a new home and taking care of the financing on that one, too. A transaction like this could amount to $100,000 in commissions to the agent. Where are that agent's loyalties?

I will discuss a case like this later in the book to show how easy it was for a real estate agent to make money while violating their fiduciary duty to their clients.

7. California Money Moves to Other States

Mortgage brokers and real estate agents were encouraging people to invest in real estate. They would hold seminars (I like to call them "Get Rich by Next Thursday" Seminars) in which they would elaborately show how the equity in their primary residence was being wasted, and that they could leverage that money by pulling out the equity and purchasing rental property in other areas. After a few years, they will have over a million dollars by doing so.

Prices, having been driven up by all of these investors, became too high in California for investors, so the same mortgage people would join companies that could do loans in other states, and began forming investment groups. They would have meetings, present properties and actually take a dozen people to places like Nevada (Las Vegas), Arizona, New Mexico, Florida and North Carolina for the sole purpose of making offers on property in those states. How did they get the money for these purchases? It was quite simple, actually. They would refinance their primary residence to make the purchases. Appreciation was now spreading across the country.

8. Where There Is Easy Money there are Crooks

Finally, the crooked people learned that they could manipulate the paperwork to literally steal from the lenders and from uneducated or naive people. In a later chapter, I will discuss a case I worked on in which a mortgage broker literally stole almost $2 million from 22 homeowners, and ruined the credit of those he recruited under the guise of helping people get out of trouble. Another case that I worked on involved identity theft, where an individual ended up owning 5 houses which he did not know he owned. The list goes on.

Yes, there were legitimate reasons for much of the appreciation in the real estate market. Unfortunately, due to the fraudulent loans and easy credit (aka, subprime); part of the increase was an illusion. The "bubble" that everyone predicted for 6 years grew from these illusionary loans, and those loans have created the downfall that is now being experienced in the real estate market place.

There are other reasons for the depth of the downturn. Just as there was artificial appreciation, there is currently artificial depreciation. Although we also experienced artificial prosperity, the recession and suffering are all too real. We will talk about that in chapter 6.

Chapter 3

The Greed and Fraud

Please remember that I am a small law office, with just myself and an assistant. If you were to take the volume of cases that I talk about in this chapter, and multiply them by the number of real estate attorneys in the United States, you will get a better understanding of how much fraud was going on out there. One must also realize that there are many fraudulent cases that were never reported, or the victims did not have the money or sophistication to hire help to protect their interests. These cases helped to lead to the inventory that should never have been constructed and loans that should never have been made.

One other thing that you should take note of is a recurring theme of the method of financing for these loans. You will see how Wall Street and the Sub-Prime lenders created the perfect tools and environment for fraud.

As you read through these cases that I was involved with, you might think that I am putting the blame on real estate and mortgage professionals.

Nothing could be further from the truth. I have many friends and colleagues in the industry who are honest and always to what is right for their clients. Many of them lost business during the 2004 – 2007 time period because they would not allow clients to purchase homes that they could not afford. Unfortunately, the clients would on many occasions be induced by those unscrupulous agents I discuss in these cases, whose primary goal was a big commission check.

I believed in real estate as a long term investment, and I gave seminars related to investment and creative financing. These seminars were directed to both real estate agents and the public interested in other forms of investment other than the stock market.

I had one seminar entitled "How to Turn $40,000 into $1.2 million." This was not a get rich quick seminar, but rather a get rich slow seminar based upon a conservative but structured investment strategy. It counted on an average 7% appreciation rate over 12 years. Part of the formula was to use Equity Sharing, in which one person lives in the property and makes the payments while the other provides the down payment. My system was a "Win-Win" formula for homeowner and investor.

Unfortunately, this process was abused and distorted by certain real estate and mortgage brokers in order to get rich quick at the expense of others, rather than for the benefit of all. Witness the first case.

CASE NUMBER 1 – The First Sign of Problems:

The first case that I became involved in stemmed from a real estate agent, also acting as a mortgage broker, who had attended one of my Creative Financing seminars. He came to me requesting that I prepare an Equity Share Agreement for use in a real estate transaction in which he would be the investor and another person would be the resident in the home and make the payments.

About six months later, I was contacted by the agent who said that he had been sued by a woman with whom he had entered into an "Equity Share" transaction. The problem was that he had tried to evict her for failure to make payments. The other problem was that an unlicensed assistant had taken the contract that I had prepared, amended it to reflect completely different terms, which were less beneficial to the resident of the property.

They had also told me that this was a purchase of a home, using the investor's money as a down payment, and the credit of the woman who was to live in the property. The reality was that the woman had already owned the property, but was facing some financial hardships, and was having difficulty in making the payments. In reality, the "investor" was taking a new loan in his name, making it look like a sale, and taking title to the property. This created a change of ownership for property tax purposes, which increased the property taxes significantly.

To make the matter even more complex, the woman who was living in the house had been in foreclosure at the time, making the entire transaction voidable. While there was some good faith by the real estate agent, because the woman would have lost the home to foreclosure had someone not stepped in, the law was on her side.

The investor/real estate agent had to pay a few thousand in legal fees, take time off to go to

43

mediation and had to address a complaint filed by the woman with the Department of Real Estate. This, along with the stress of being involved in a lawsuit, was all the result of attempting to "get rich quick" by the investor and the loan broker. Fortunately for everyone, this all occurred at a time when the market was still rising, and ultimately, the property was sold and everyone walked away with at least some money and a minimum of damage.

The previous case was the first step toward using the straw buyer. Instead of doing an equity share agreement, the "buyer" would purchase the house and allow the "seller" to remain in the property and make the payments under what was supposed to be a rental agreement. 95% of the time, the sellers were unable to make the payments, and the buyer would evict them, taking the house over for less than the fair market value of the property.

CASE NUMBER 2 – The Straw Buyer:

This was the first case I encountered regarding a "Straw Buyer," and started in 2005. A straw buyer is a person who purchases a house of an individual who is in financial trouble, or on the verge of foreclosure, with the idea that it will be returned to the Seller.

The house was old and dilapidated, and the owner was in his late 70's. He also had a wife in her mid 40's. They were a few days away from the Trustee Sale of the property. Two people who worked at a mortgage brokerage company came to their home and offered to buy the property from them, rent it back to them, help them to clean up their credit, and

44

then sell it back to them. Neither of these people held a real estate license.

They used the credit of the girl friend of one of the individuals (because he had already done this a couple of times and could not qualify for another loan), and the other one processed the loan through the company he worked for. They did 100% financing, paid the mortgage company exorbitant fees due to the yield spreads, paid the other person $40,000 "for repairs", much of which was paid to the girlfriend for the use of her credit. In essence, approximately $70,000 was stripped from the equity of the property, with the balance of the equity being paid to the sellers.

The forty-nine year old wife of the old man got hold of the proceeds from the "sale" and disappeared; leaving the old man in the house under a rental agreement that he could not afford with only his Social Security. When he didn't pay the rent, they gave him a three day notice to pay or quit, and tried to evict him. He found an attorney who would help him, and he filed suit to have the entire transaction rescinded. He named the "Buyer", the two other individuals, the broker and the lender who provided the funding and the title company.

The lender and the title company both buried the other attorney in paperwork, delaying the process for months. The mortgage broker did not have E&O insurance to cover the actions of his employees, and had to pay for an attorney himself to defend the action. Thousands were spent on attorney fees.

A year and a half later, the old man was forced to leave his home and received small settlements from some of the individuals. His younger wife, who had absconded with the proceeds of the sale, blew the money on drugs and alcohol, and ended up in rehab with nothing left.

The interesting thing is that the property was basically worthless. The house was next to the Russian River in Northern California and was old in need of repair. The septic system was shot, and could not be replaced without spending thousands of dollars relocating it further from the river. If the house was torn down, I am not sure if a new structure could ever be built on the lot because of its proximity to the river.

These wise investors lost thousands of dollars because of their greed, and even if there had been no lawsuit, would have lost thousands on the property.

These types of straw buyer "deals" were becoming more and more prevalent.

The next case is one that I briefly mentioned earlier in which a real estate agent had the possibility of having five transactions riding on the sale of one house.

CASE NUMBER 3 – Real Estate Agent Greed:

As I mentioned in an earlier chapter, two things helped create the mess in which we find ourselves. First is that anyone with a four year college degree could take the California Real Estate Broker's Exam, and open a real estate office and hire and manage real estate agents without having ever done a real estate transaction themselves. Having taken the Broker's Exam, I can guarantee you that it is not that difficult to pass and in no way tests the actual requirements of operating a real estate office.

The second issue was the ability of real estate agents to also act as the mortgage broker for the same client that they were representing in the purchase of sale of the house. This leads me to Case number three.

I was contacted by a real estate agent whose client was being sued by the purchaser of her client's house. As it turns out, the real estate agent and her broker were also being sued by the buyer. As it further turns out, the real estate agent, who was originally licensed in 2003, also represented the buyer. Here's what happened (some information coming from Agent and some coming from the allegations of Buyer):

Agent listed the property for sale and listed it on the Multiple Listing Service. The Agent was holding an open house one weekend afternoon, when Buyer came into the house. Buyer loved the house, and wanted to buy it, but had to wait for the house she was selling to close escrow. Buyer also claimed that she did not like the agent she had selling her house, and wanted Agent to write up the contract to purchase this house. Agent agreed, and wrote up the offer for full price.

A few days later, Buyer told Agent that she was having trouble getting a loan, and wanted to know if Agent knew anyone who could help her. Agent told her not to worry, because she was a mortgage broker, too. She would get the financing that Buyer needed so she could purchase the home. Agent now has three transactions (one sale, one purchase and one loan) from which she will "earn" a commission.

Buyer did not want to pay for a formal property inspection (according to Agent) because she had numerous friends in the construction business because of her own business, and instead had a contractor come through to do and inspection without a written report. Buyer did not obtain any other form of inspection.

When the first appraiser came out to the property, the property did not appraise at the purchase price. Agent sent out a second appraiser (without notifying Buyer) who did appraise it at full price. The appraiser was Agent's brother. It was noted that there was a stairway to the back door, and that it was totally dilapidated and suffering from dry rot to the wood. The bank, as a condition of funding the loan, required that the stairs be replaced. Buyer, according to Agent, said that she was planning to totally rebuild the back stairs with a deck, authorized agent to have someone build an inexpensive staircase so the escrow could close, and then she would tear it down and rebuild the deck that she wanted after escrow closed. Agent hired a "handyman" who was not a licensed contractor who rebuilt the stairs. He also replaced a few planks on the front stairs, which were also rotted out.

While all of this is going on, Agent helped Seller find a new house to purchase, contingent on the sale of Seller's home to Buyer, and of course obtained the new financing for them, too. Now, Agent has five transactions (One Sale, two Purchases, and two Loans) on which she would "earn" a commission. Conservatively, that came to about $100,000.00 dependant on the successful close of escrow of the Seller's house to the Buyer. But all is going well, until ....

Buyer contacts Agent to inform her that due to various circumstances related to the sale of Buyer's house, she will not have enough cash for the down payment to complete the purchase of Seller's house, a shortage of about $30,000.00. Agent has way too much at stake to allow a little thing like $30,000.00 stand in her way of receiving $100,000.00, so she offers to loan $30,000 to Buyer so they can close all of the escrows. Of course, the lender would not allow Agent to loan money to the Buyer, so she drafts a "Gift Letter" stating that the money is a gift from Buyer's mother to the Buyer, and has the mother sign it.

The letter is forwarded to the lender, who accepts it, the escrows all close, Buyer has her new home, Seller has their new home and Agent has $100,000.00 and a promissory note for another $30,000.00.

The problem arises when Buyer finds more problems with the house than what was discovered by her contractor friend, and that she has now determined that it would cost her $150,000 to correct all of the problems. Agent starts demanding repayment of the $30,000.00 promissory note, which Buyer cannot pay. Buyer consults with an attorney, and a lawsuit is filed by Buyer against Agent, Agent's broker and the Seller. This sale closed in July of 2005, and is still going on in the courts in California. That commission will disappear long before this case is ever brought to a conclusion.

This case was the first where I witnessed the wholesale fraud and deception by a mortgage broker in which he literally stole millions of dollars from less than two dozen homeowners.

CASE NUMBER 4 – The Criminal Element:

This next case was one that ended up in the criminal courts in Oakland, California in 2005, based on transactions that took place in late 2004 and early 2005. The mortgage broker involved stripped more than $3 million in equity from 21 homes and homeowners in about a 6 month span of time.

Following is a description of how he did it, but don't try this at home, because it could end you up in jail:

1. He would find people who were either in desperate need of money, but unable to qualify for a refinance because of credit scores, or people who were already in foreclosure and facing the loss of their home (in a still appreciating market).

2. He would go to these people and explain that he had a program to help them keep their homes. He would find someone (he called them "Investors") who would "purchase" their home (the Straw Buyer), he would help them repair their credit, and then help them buy the home back a year later.

3. He informed them that the "purchaser" would obtain a loan in the amount sufficient to pay off existing loans and to pay the "purchaser" $10,000.00 for the use of their credit. He would also take out the equivalent of 12 months of payment, which the "purchaser" would use to make the monthly payments. That way, the homeowner would be able to stay in the house without making payments for a year. Whatever money the homeowner needed would also be taken out and given to the "seller" homeowner.

4. The mortgage broker would then go out and recruit the Straw Buyers with the lure of making a quick $10,000 without having to make any payments. He persuaded them with the idea of "helping someone who otherwise could lose their home." He also said that, if the homeowner did not repurchase the house after a year, they could start charging rent.

Does it sound too good to be true? Of course it was, because there were serious flaws to the plan, even if it was above board.

The first thing that would go wrong is that, in California, the sale of the property would trigger a change in property taxes. A homeowner, who had a tax basis of $100,000 because they had owned the home so long, would have their annual property tax go from $1,400 a year to as much as $6,000 per year.

Ultimately, the home owner would be required to buy back the house with a new loan, which they probably would not qualify for, in an amount much higher than what they had owed before the transaction.

To make matters worse, the mortgage broker would charge high rates and fees, again through yield spreads, and sometimes charged a sales commission of 5-6% on a sham transaction which was not really a sale.

That was not enough for this greedy character. He would process the loans, not at the amount that was needed to accomplish what he told the home owner was the amount needed, but instead he obtained financing for 100% of the value of the property. Then he convinced the title company, with either a fraudulent or unknowing authorization from the "seller", that the title company should disburse all of the funds to him, and that he would distribute the proceeds accordingly.

After he distributed the funds to the Straw Buyer and the home owner, he retained the remainder for himself. In all, his take on 21 properties was in excess of $1 million.

I became involved in this case by representing three of the Investors who were each named in separate lawsuits by the victims. There were 21 separate lawsuits, and because it was a criminal matter, the judge for the criminal court in Oakland attempted to arrange for a global settlement of all of the claims. The end result was that most of the Investors had little money and many filed bankruptcy, and the title companies involved had either paid a small settlement or had filed bankruptcy and closed their doors. These cases that started in 2005 were not finally dismissed until late in 2009. Of course, during that time frame, the values of the properties dropped by 50% or more.

The clown who pulled off this scam ended up doing a plea bargain in which he pled guilty to one count of fraud. Of course he was stripped of his real estate license, but he ended up doing one year in county jail and 5 years of probation. The District Attorney said that, although they could have convicted him of multiple counts of fraud and sentenced him to more time in state prison, he believed that he would have been set free earlier because of the overcrowding of the prison system and the fact that this was a "white collar crime." He felt that the county could and would keep a better eye on him than the State of California would.

At the time I was working this case, I read about a similar case in Southern California, where the mortgage broker pulled the same swindle against more than a hundred homeowners. How were they able to pull these off?

1. Greed on behalf of everyone ... the broker, the investor, the title company, the lender, and even the homeowner in some cases.
2. The liar loans. Good FICO score, stated income, no verification.
3. Lack of supervision by the broker, partly because they had no idea what they were doing.
4. The corruption of the American Dream

The next case is one caused by people trusting people on the basis that they were of the same culture. I reported this case and the broker involve to the Contra Costa County District Attorney's office. He politely told me to send in the paperwork, and he would be able to get to it in about six months. His workload of real estate fraud cases had mushroomed.

He also mentioned to me that he previously worked in Vice and thought he had seen it all. Drugs and prostitution was nothing in compared to what he saw in real estate fraud. In vice, the wrongdoers were often also the victims. He said that in real estate fraud, people were losing their life savings and property to the perpetrators.

CASE NO. 5 – Taking Advantage of the Uneducated and Trusting:

One thing that began occurring was that cultures started relying on members of their own culture to help them with the purchase of real estate. It seemed that Spanish speaking people dealt with

Spanish Speaking agents; those from China with Chinese agents, the Philippines, Koreans, etc. all dealt with people who were originally from their counties and spoke their languages. The problem was that the real estate contracts were written in English, and many real estate agents and brokers took advantage of those who could not speak the language.

I call this Case No. 5, but there were actually 2 cases involving the same real estate agent/mortgage broker who took advantage of two of my clients who were basically Spanish speaking, although they had some understanding of English.

In the first case, Mr. and Mrs. Santos (not their real names and they went by different last names) owned a house which they had purchased using her brother's credit. They had put the money down and made all of the payments, but because their credit was marginal at the time, they bought the house with the help of her brother.

After a few years, they decided that they wanted to move to a bigger house, and started looking with an agent who spoke Spanish. Their credit was better, and they were going to be able to sell their home for what they thought was a substantial profit.

The real estate agent, who also did mortgages, told them that he liked their house and would like to purchase it as an investment. He offered them enough money so that they would have 20% down for the purchase of the new house. The problem is that what he offered them was about $60,000 of what the property was actually worth. On top of that, he charged them a standard "commission" for the sale of the property, even though it never went on the market and he didn't do any work. Since they did not understand the closing papers, they did not even realize that the price for the property was under value and that he had charged them a commission.

He then obtained financing for them under Mr. Santos' name only to purchase the new house, which included a prepayment penalty in order for the agent to be paid the highest possible commission from the lender.

About 14 months later, Mr. and Mrs. Santos wanted to pull some equity out of their house, partly because they thought they would have had more after they sold. They still did not realize what the agent had done to them. This time, the agent told them that pulling cash out through a refinance was very difficult, and that Mr. Santos should instead "sell" the house to his wife. The value of the house had gone up significantly, and it was now worth about $100,000 more than the original purchase price.

When all was said and done, the owners received about $35,000 in cash while their mortgage balance went up by more than $80,000.00! How did this happen? They were required to pay a pre-payment penalty on the previous loan and the agent charged more fees, resulting in more than $45,000 of the equity being stripped from them and given to the agent and his broker.

They had believed, at the time of the last refinance, that they would be receiving more cash than the actually received, and therefore ran out much earlier than they had originally anticipated. They called the agent one more time to pull more cash from the property.

He gave them the same story about how difficult it was to pull money from the equity of the property through a refinance. Since they could not "sell" the property to the husband again, because it would show up on the title report, the agent recommended that the property be "sold" *to the agent's wife!*

Believe it or not, they agreed to this scheme and did a "sale" to the agent's wife in order for them to get a few thousand dollars again. Shortly after this transaction was completed, someone told Mr. and Mrs. Santos that they no longer owned the house, because it was in the name of the Agent's wife.

They demanded that the house be returned to their name, so one more sale was created where the house was sold again from the agent's wife to Mr. Santos. The loan on the house was now about $560,000 on a house that they originally purchased for $300,000. Mr. and Mrs. Santo received a total of about $90,000 of that equity, while the difference went to real estate commissions, prepayment penalties, escrow and title fees and other loan fees. On top of that, the property taxes doubled from about $3100 per year to over $6,000 per year because of the "sale" transactions.

After filing a lawsuit and attending two mediations, Mr. and Mrs. Santos received a settlement of about $225,000 before attorney fees. They lost the home to foreclosure and ended up getting divorced.

In the second case involving this agent, Ricardo, the brother of Mrs. Santos was the victim. As you may remember, he was the actual owner of the first house that Mr. and Mrs. Santos lived in, but he had actually only provided his credit in order for his sister to have a house.

In early 2006, the agent approached Ricardo and told him that he had a good client who needed a co-signer for a loan, and that if Ricardo would co-sign for this client, that the agent would pay $5,000 to Ricardo from the commissions he earned. Ricardo made about $32,000 a year, so $5,000 was very enticing for him. He also felt that he was helping someone. Ricardo had a great FICO score, and proceeded to give the agent all of his credit information. About a month later, the agent presented Ricardo with a check for $5,000.

Approximately 4 months later, Ricardo started receiving phone calls about mortgage payments that were late. He tried calling the agent, but he would never return the phone calls. He finally told someone who had some knowledge of the real estate, and they went to the County Recorder's office to review the records. What they found was five single family residences in Ricardo's name, all purchased within 2-3 months of each other!

Now here was a man who was making $32K per year, who now had mortgage payments in excess of $20,000 per month. How can someone purchase five houses in someone else's name, with monthly payments of 2/3 of what they were earning without the individual knowing about it and a lender approving it? It was actually very simple. The lenders were never the same, the loans were all stated income "liar loans" and the agent's son was a Notary Public who was able to notarize all of the deed of trust documents, even though they were never signed by Ricardo.

The agent and his son made thousands of dollars in fees on the loans, perhaps commissions on the purchases, and probably hoped that they market would continue to go up so that they could sell the properties for a profit, tax free. After all, any tax ramifications would have ultimately gone to Ricardo, because his name was on the title and the loans. I guess they did not believe that there would ever be a way to track this all back to them.

Ricardo's main initial concern was to have the loan information removed from his credit record. After filing police reports, complaints with the county District Attorney's Office and Identity Theft documents with the lenders, not one of them would remove the delinquent reports from his credit record. A lawsuit had already been filed against the agent and his broker regarding these transactions, so we added the lenders as defendants through an amended complaint. Eventually, three of the lenders executed stipulated agreements whereby they were dismissed from the case and agreed to remove any reference from Ricardo's credit. He also received a small settlement from the Broker's insurance company. In the mean time, he had to wait almost 3 years to get the matter resolved, and he still receives threats occasionally from collection agencies demanding payment on the seconds.

All five of the houses were foreclosed, two of the lenders filed for bankruptcy, and one (Washington Mutual) was seized by FDIC and give (the government calls it sold) to J.P. Morgan – Chase. Just as J.P. Morgan personally did in 1906, the bank that now bears his name was swooping up banks and making itself bigger and more powerful than ever.

In the mean time, people like Ricardo continued to suffer.

Of course, the recurring thing in all of these cases was that there was the greed of wanting to make money at the expense of others, and the tools were provided by the lenders and Wall Street to enable these people to pull off these frauds. Sub-prime, stated income loans were involved in each and every one of these cases. I can guarantee you that if these types of loans were not in existence; the individuals involved would never have been able to pull off these scams.

The other thing, which is not as apparent in these cases on the surface, was that all of the agents or mortgage brokers involved had their licenses for less than four years, with many less than two years. All but one worked for brokers who provided no training or supervision and had also been in the business for a short period of time.

Chapter 4

The Fall

When and why did "The Fall" begin? It is very simple. When interest rates started going up, it meant that the source of money described earlier in the book was starting to dry up. Credit became a little tighter. There had been issues getting some of the subprime loans that had been issued refinanced, which was the pattern of most of these types of lenders.

A home buyer would get a subprime loan with a teaser rate of 2.9% with payments fixed at that rate for one or two years. The actual interest rate, however, would be something in the range of 7%, and the unpaid interest would accrue. Often, the borrower would be given a choice of what he wanted to pay. He could pay the fixed payment rate, an interest only rate, a fully amortized rate, and even a rate that would pay off the loan in 15 years. Since the borrower couldn't afford the higher payments, they just paid the minimum and their principle balance continued to go up.

The increase in the balance was no problem, because property values were appreciating at a rate far above what the loan balance was becoming. At the end of first year or two, the loan payment would adjust to whatever the current rate might be. The mortgage brokers told the borrower that there would be no problem with that, because they would just refinance the loan, and in some cases, they could pull out additional cash to buy an investment property or a boat, new car or other toy. Each time a mortgage broker refinanced someone, he made money.

Lenders made $640 billion in subprime loans in 2006, nearly twice the level just three years earlier, according to *Inside B&C Lending*, which tracks the mortgage business.

The Mortgage Bankers Association said that subprime loans amounted to about 20 percent of the nation's mortgage lending and about 17 percent of home purchases in 2006. Financial firms and hedge funds at the time probably owned more than $1 trillion in securities backed by subprime mortgages.

The mortgage bankers group reported in early March, 2007 that about 13 percent of subprime loans were then delinquent, more than five times the delinquency rate for home loans to borrowers with top credit. In addition, more than 2 percent of subprime loans had foreclosure proceedings start in the fourth quarter. The pyramid scheme was starting to collapse.

In April, 2007, New Century Mortgage, which was the second largest subprime lender, having made $51.6 billion in subprime loans in 2006, filed for bankruptcy and immediately laid off 3,200 employees. This sent shockwaves throughout the financial market, because New Century owed $8.4 billion to companies such as Bank of America, Morgan Stanley, Citigroup, Barclays Bank and UBS. Of course, they were just the beginning.

Soon, the bonds backed by subprime mortgages were downgraded in their ratings. In August, 2007, two funds managed by Bear Stearns that were expose to the subprime market filed for bankruptcy. In September, the Federal Reserve begins cutting interest rates to banks. In October Merrill Lynch, UBS and Citigroup reveal that they have suffered subprime losses and billions of securities backed by home loans are again downgraded.

In November, 2007 the announcement of losses from subprime loans comes from Bank of America, Morgan Stanley, Wachovia, HSBC, Barclays and Freddie Mac. That was followed in December with the Fed, closing the barn door after the horses had all escaped, tightening the subprime lending rules.

In January, 2008, Bank of America buys troubled Countrywide whose sole business model was to control the mortgage industry in the United States, and had used subprime loans as its main catalyst for achieving that goal.

In March, 2008 Bear Stearns, and 85 year old Investment Bank was sold to JPMorgan Chase in order to avert a bankruptcy by the company. The sale was backed by the Fed and partially paid for by the taxpayers.

In July, 2008 the FDIC took over subprime lender IndyMac and in September, 2008 they seized the assets of Washington Mutual and sold them to JPMorgan Chase, while the FDIC (and the taxpayers) assumed much of their liabilities.

During the time frame starting in January, 2000 and ending in December, 2006, a total of 24 banks were seized and sold by the FDIC. Beginning in January, 2007 and ending in December, 2010 a total of 325 banks have been seized and either sold or managed by FDIC. Most were acquired by other banks, but a very few were slowly allowed to close by FDIC.

This was partly the result of the meltdown, but part of the cause rests with the surviving lenders, servicers and state and Federal Governments. I get ahead of myself, and we will save that cause for Chapter 6. First, I want to address short sales in the next chapter.

Chapter 5

The Short Sale Syndrome

Before becoming an attorney, I worked as an active real estate agent and broker. The key word in this sentence is "worked," because there were no gift loans that could be obtained by writing in a salary a part time occupation that was never verified by the lender. There was always a lender and, if the down payment was less than 20%, a private mortgage insurance company who insured the lender on the portion in excess of 80% loan to value.

The one thing that I learned in my years of selling real estate was that real estate had nothing to do with homes; it had everything to do with financing. Realistically, there were few people who could or would pay cash for a home. There were incentives, such as mortgage interest and property tax deductions on ones tax return, which made it advantageous to borrow a large portion of the cost of the house. The result was that a buyer had to qualify for a loan for a certain amount before he could go look at homes within his price range.

Those all changed with subprime loans, because now a buyer could find a house he liked first, and then manipulate the loan application to reflect an amount of income needed to qualify for the loan. As I mentioned earlier, prices were mushrooming, not because of actual prosperity in the country, but because loans were cheap and easy to get, and there seemed to be an endless supply of money as so many investors jumped onto the mortgage backed security train.

Suddenly, the available money well started to dry up, and loans became harder to obtain. Many with subprime loans could not refinanced, as their mortgage brokers had promised they could, and were faced with an adjustment of their interest rates and loan payments to a level that they would not be able to meet. They put their homes on the market at a price that would enable them to walk away without any money, but without owing anyone, either. The problem was, there was no money to loan and the Fed had tightened up the lending rules.

As the availability of money started dropping, so did the number of sales and the sales prices. Those who had some equity could drop their prices and sell their homes if they had to, while those with no equity could not. Those who could not sell for enough to cover their loans and sales costs would end up in foreclosure. The banks, who had created loan programs that had never been seen before in a downturn, decided to handle the issue in the same way that they had done for hundreds of years. FORECLOSE.

Soon, some learned that, since they were having trouble getting rid of their inventory, it might be better to allow the owner to sell the house for less than what was owed and either write off the difference or accept an unsecured note for the payment of the difference. Depending on the type of loan and the state in which the property was, many lenders had no right to seek a deficiency judgment for whatever would be lost.

Short sales were not new, but as it turns out, they never had been used to the extent that they were going to be used starting in 2007. Basically, a "Short Sale" is created where the property is sold for less than the amount of the loan. If there is only one lender, the issue can be addressed fairly easily. The lender agrees to a bottom line number and upon payment of that amount, they release their lien to the property, and everyone went on their merry way.

The problems arose when, as with many of the loans that were in existence, there was a first and a second loan that were made without any down payment by the borrower (100% loan). In the beginning, the first mortgage holder was fairly secure, and it was the second mortgage holder that had to negotiate the reduction in its loan. They were reluctant to do so in the beginning, and foreclosures continued.

Now, take a minute and think about whom gets hurt in a foreclosure other than the lender and the homeowner. How about the real estate agent, the title and escrow companies, the inspection companies, and all of the other businesses that support the real estate industry. The title companies, who for years prior to the demise of the real estate market, had sponsored seminars on how to use your equity to invest in property, now began sponsoring seminars training agents how to effectively handle a short sale. Short sales became the name of the game.

Unfortunately, the term "Short Sale" was an oxymoron, in that these transactions usually took 3-4 months for the lenders to give an approval for a transaction. They wanted a hardship letter, financials of the borrower, tax returns, and on and on. Usually, if the borrower was continuing to make his payments, the lender would ultimately come back with a negative response. In many cases, while the lender was reviewing the documents, the prices of homes in the area would drop to a level that was below the price originally offered, and the buyer would cancel the escrow and buy another home nearby for less money.

There were also situations where the lender would get information that would show whether or not they could enforce a deficiency judgment against the borrower if they foreclosed.

There were also tax ramifications to a short sale that agents did not understand. Whatever the lender did not receive was considered a cancellation of debt by the IRS, and taxable as ordinary income, as if he had actually received the money. Eventually, statutes were enacted that would relieve some of that debt, but in many cases where the properties had been refinanced and cash taken out, the borrowers were hit by this additional tax. There were other exceptions, such as insolvency, but if there was not exemption, there would be a tax on top of all the other misery that these sellers faced.

Even today, there are "short sale specialists" who will cave into every demand by a lender before the lender will consider a short sale. It still can take months for a lender to approve a short sale, and there are still outrageous demands made by those in second position, even though they would never receive anything if the first mortgage holder was to foreclose.

It seems that the more you give them, the longer it takes to complete the process. Why do short sale and mortgage modification requests, which I will talk about later, negotiations take so long? As you will read later in this book, it is because the servicing companies make more money the longer things are delayed.

My recommendation to people now is to tell the lenders that they are not going to give them any information about themselves. There are only a few things that the lender really needs to know to make an informed decision:

1. What is the current value of the property?
2. What is and how strong is the offer for the property?
3. An idea of what the current inventory is in the area.
4. That the borrower is not going to make any more payments, and that the lender can accept this offer or foreclose.

Of course, the servicing companies hate this tactic. I had a client who owned a vacant lot in what was supposed to be a high end development the area. The developer, who still owned 46 lots in the development, had been served with a cease and desist order by the Department of Real Estate because he had failed to complete the amenities that were promised in the original offering, and was at that time more than $325,000 behind in payment of HOA dues on those lots. He was more than $100,000 behind when my client purchased his lot, a fact that was not disclosed. Furthermore, the developer sold off approximately 237 acres of what was supposed to be open space within the development to a third party who was planning to develop that land for smaller lots and homes.

The prices plummeted and eventually the property, which was originally $490,000, had dropped in value to less than $150,000 against a loan amount of $283,000. When my client learned of the non-disclosure, he filed suit against the developer, the HOA, the seller and his real estate agent. He also notified the lender, JPMorgan Chase, originally a Washington Mutual loan, that there was a lawsuit going on based on fraud and that he would be discontinuing payments. He also agreed to return the property to them in the form of a deed in lieu of foreclosure, allowing them to sell it before the prices really fell. He never received a reply from Chase.

He tried to sell the property, and after almost 18 months, with no payments having been made in that time, received an all cash offer of $150,000. The agent for my client contacted the bank regarding the short sale, and they sent out their normal "short sale" package demanding a letter of hardship, bank statements, tax returns and copies of W-2s. I contacted the person who was assigned the task of gathering all of this information before the package could be forwarded to a "negotiator." I explained to her that none of that information would be forthcoming, and that the only things they needed to know was:

1. That the offer was for $150,000 in cash, no loan.
2. That the last sale that took place 11 months earlier was in the amount of $100,000.

3. That there were 8 lots on the market at the time of our conversation, meaning there was at least a 7 year inventory.
4. That there was a cease and desist order against the developer and that the developer was by then $500,000 past due on HOA dues.
5. That a hard money lender was only months away from foreclosing on the remaining 45 lots owned by the developer, which would dramatically increase the inventory.
6. That my client was not going to make any more payments, and
7. That there was a foreclosure scheduled within a few weeks, and if they did not accept the offer, they would own the property soon anyway.

The clerk whose responsibility it was to gather all of the information said to me, "I can't guarantee that I can get a negotiator to look at this without that information." I responded that my client does not care if it goes to a negotiator or not, and that he was actually helping Chase by even allowing it to be considered as a short sale. Next thing you know, my client gets a call from the agent who tells him that the file had gone to a negotiator.

Unfortunately, I had forgotten something I learned in trying to help someone get a mortgage modification. Very simply put, the fact is that "you can't fight stupid." With all of the information that had been provided to them, which included a list of the properties for sale and sold in the past 3 years, the brilliant negotiator from Chase decided that the property was worth at least $175,000 and that they would not accept less than $165,000, and that all of the past due HOA dues for the lot (my client quit paying them when he filed the lawsuit) had to be paid by my client or the buyer. The buyer refused the counter offer, and walked away.

Chase eventually proceeded with the foreclosure, and on the Trustee Deed document showed the value to be $143,000.00. Perhaps they were trying to get their property taxes lower.

I have also had clients who had offers that were in excess of the listed price of other homes in the neighborhood, which were turned down by the lender and foreclosed upon a few days later. There was just no logic to what was being done.

Short sales are far from over. As I will demonstrate in the next chapter, the lenders and servicing companies have driven the prices down to a point that people are refusing to continue to make payments on homes that are now worth $200-300K less that the amount of their loans. They realize that it will take longer to get their lost equity back than it will for their credit rating to be repaired. These are not people with subprime loans, either. These are people who had "A" paper loans with good down payments, who just see no future in retaining ownership of such a losing proposition as the home they were living in.

What goes around comes around, and the lenders are going to continue to take losses from short sales and foreclosures for years to come.

Chapter 6

The Meltdown

We have had downturns in the economy and drops in real estate values in the past. Why did it become so severe this time? As I mentioned in the last chapter, the lenders tried to handle the problem in the same manner that they had handled delinquent mortgages in the past. Demand payment, file the necessary papers to start the foreclosure process, foreclose, get the property sold so that it in no longer in your "non-performing" asset books and keep on operating. Sure, there could be some losses, but this is how we have always handled things in the past, and that is how they were going to handle it now.

Of course, the banks and other lenders had created this monster with their loan products and it was those loan products that had eliminated the cushion that they had enjoyed in the past. More foreclosures and more short sales led to the same thing: further and deeper erosion of the real estate market and the value of real estate.

One city in California, Antioch, which is a suburb of the San Francisco/Oakland metropolitan area, had experienced rapid population growth and development of new "affordable" housing tracts. The greed started with the city government because their idea of raising revenue was to get more homes built and collect their portion of the property taxes, along with Mello-Roos assessments. The developer's greed came with the construction of the biggest houses that they could build on the smallest lot possible. The cost of land was more than the cost of construction in many areas. The greed of potential homebuyers came out by "needing" larger homes than they needed or could actually afford, and be willing to drive 60-100 miles each day to work. Finally, the greed of the lenders, as well as some mortgage brokers and real estate agents, continued to drive up the prices.

In January, 2007, the median price home in the City of Antioch was $550,000. As of November, 2010 it had plummeted to $200,000, a 70% drop in value. How could this have happened?

Well, it started with the fact that many of the people who purchased homes in Antioch were less sophisticated and usually marginal credit ratings. They were enamored by the large, new homes that they could "afford" and the image it would portray, without taking into consideration the number of miles and hours that they would spend on the road each day. Many were suckered in by the low payment, easy qualifying loans that were available to them. In some cases, they had no idea that the mortgage brokers had lied on the loan applications to show that they were earning more than they actually did.

When the credit tightened up, many of these home owners could no longer refinance with new liar loans, and were faced with the adjustment in the payments on their loans which they could no longer afford to pay. In actuality, the never could afford the homes that they had purchased, other than through the "smoke and mirror" loans. They would put their homes on the market for what they owed, plus the selling costs, but there were no buyers because there were no loans available. Remember what I said in the last chapter; the real estate market has nothing to do with houses; it has everything to do with financing. No financing equals no sales.

So, one of these homeowners is unable to make his payments for three months and the lender files a Notice of Default, waits 120 days, holds the trustee sale and now owns the property. Lenders do not want real estate in their portfolio, so the put the house on the market at a price below the market rate in order to get a quick sale. Let's say that the market price is $550,000 for a specific property, but the lender sells it for $500,000. One house sold at that price does not have much impact on the overall market value, but soon another homeowner is unable to make his payments and that house is also foreclosed and sold for $500,000. Now, appraiser must take those into consideration, and sellers are forced to drop their list prices for a similar home to that $500,000 level. The problem is that they owe more than that, and are now forced to do a short sale.

The cycle continues as short sales are denied by the servicing companies and/or the lenders, and foreclosures continue. However, the banks are unable to sell the properties for the market price of $500,000 because there is still no financing and an increasing inventory. They drop the price to $450,000 to get them sold. This downward spiral continues as the number of defaults and foreclosures continue, and the non-performing inventory builds up in the portfolios of the lenders. Now people who had equity at one time and had good loans with sufficient down payments find themselves owning a house that has a value less than what they owe.

Because the construction industry died, many of the people living in these areas lost their jobs. That downturn in the economy led to the layoffs of the unskilled workers. Support people jobs in the real estate industry, such as escrow officers, inspectors, mortgage processors, were also being laid off. As jobs went away, so did the ability of these people to make payments on their loans go away. The ripple effect of these layoffs contributed to the increase in defaults and foreclosures against these individuals.

The artificial prosperity that this country once enjoyed had come to an end. Many people used the increasing equity in their homes to live above their means by taking out equity loans to pay for that new truck or SUV, buying a boat or taking that expensive vacation to Australia. The money that had been available from those equity lines of credit had been artificially feeding America's and the world's economy for ten years. Now, everything came to a screeching halt, and the unemployment numbers and the foreclosures continued to climb.

The lenders cut their own throats as well through the deluge of foreclosures. Remember, the companies that made the original loans, such as Countrywide, had packaged these loans into a large trust, had the packages rated as AAA investments and then sold shares of the trusts as mortgage backed securities. Let's imagine that there were a thousand loans of $500,000 each in one of these trusts. That means the original package was worth $500 million.

One foreclosure doesn't really have an effect on the complete value of the portfolio, because the true value was in the cash flow that the portfolio was generating. Each of these portfolios was generating $250,000 per month, although in many cases this was through accrued interest and not actual payments. But no one cared because real estate always goes up in value.

However, the mass of foreclosures and the resulting reduction in the fair market value of the properties began driving the value of the portfolio down. When the market value of the homes dropped to $400,000, the value of the portfolio dropped to $400 million, a $100 million reduction. As the market values of the houses dropped, the number of new defaults increased, which reduced the cash flow that each of these packages was generating. The increased value due to accrued interest was not matching the decrease in the overall package. Overall cash flow also was considerably reduced.

The carnage had started and no one, lender, servicer, or government was making any realistic effort to stem the tide. It became an avalanche. Once the first pack of snow started slipping, it took out everything in its path.

I won't bother going into statistics, but suffice it to say that the states that suffered the most were the ones that had experienced the most growth. California, Florida, Las Vegas and Arizona were among the hardest hit. These were the states that were highlighted in the investment seminars and where many people from California took their money to invest in real estate with the hope of making a million dollars in 1-2 years. These areas suffered the most, along with many areas in the Midwest, such as

Michigan, which were affected by high unemployment in automobile and other manufacturing.

Was there a housing bubble? Absolutely, just as there had been stock market bubbles, the dot com bubble, gold bubbles, crude oil bubbles, etc. Most bubbles are fueled, not by sound investments, but by trying to get rich quick. The problem with that is that the ones who helped start the bubble are the ones who know when to bail out and bet against the bubble.

That is what Goldman-Sachs did when they were selling mortgage backed securities through one division and betting against them with other clients through another division.

While some real estate markets are showing signs of recovery, others are still floundering and could be facing another dip as the 5-Year ARMS (Adjustable Rate Mortgages) begin adjusting. At this time, the adjustments may actually provide borrowers with lower payments. However, as indexes increase, so will the interest rate, and the payments could become unmanageable for some.

The meltdown will continue for some.

Chapter 7

The Mortgage Modification Mania

I am not sure how it started, but all of a sudden Mortgage Modification became the big thing, or should I say scam. I am not sure if the banks were starting to panic because of the increase in defaults or the increase in their inventory. Were they finally beginning to learn that it would be better to start getting something by modifying the payment terms rather than taking back property and selling it for a loss? Or was it another way to make money based upon the fear and lack of sophistication of some of the home owners?

In early September of 2008 I was approached by someone who was involved in a coaching group for mortgage people. The sponsors of the group were giving an online seminar to try to help mortgage professionals to begin making money again by helping people get their mortgages modified. I listened in on the webinar and found it to be interesting. About two weeks later, I attended the California State Bar convention in Monterey, California and attended a seminar conducted by attorneys who were discussing the Sub-Prime mortgage mess and mortgage modification was part of the discussion.

I found it interesting that one of the attorneys who was a presenter in the seminar had been General Counsel with such subprime lenders such as New Century and Option One (an affiliate of Lehman Brothers Bank). She was now helping people with mortgage modifications and claims to have been successful. Perhaps it was because she knew some back alleys.

It sounded like a good way to take part in helping home owners, the lenders and the economy by getting the loans modified for people, thus enabling the lenders to turn non-producing loans into producing loans and stemming the tide of foreclosures. Hang on to that dream.

I began working with a group of mortgage brokers who had tried to help people refinance their loans and reduce their payments. Since there was no credit available, they were unsuccessful. They referred those people to me, and I put together a package to present to lenders that would give them the basis for modifying payments to the level we were requesting and to show them the amount of losses that the investor of the loan would have in comparison to modifying the loan in one of two ways. One way would be to reduce the principle of the loan and keep the same interest rate, which I knew that no one would do at that time. The second method, which provided the lender with income and maintained the loan balance, would have provided an income to the investor.

The following chart demonstrated to the servicing company the amount of the loan, any past due interest or deferred interest (if it was a negative amortized loan) the payments, the fully indexed payments, taxes and insurance, and what the loan balance would have been in five years if all of these payments were made. I then showed what the current market value was, the cost of foreclosing, holding the property and the selling expenses, not including past due property taxes. The amount of loss to the investor in this example would have exceeded $280,000.

First Loan Principle	**491000.00**
Past Due Interest	**75000.00**
Deferred Interest	**0.00**
Total Balance	566000.00
Current Payment - 1st	**2767.15**
Interest Rate - 1st	**6.750%**
Full Index Pmt - 1st	**3671.07**
Taxes and Insurance	4890.00
Loan Balance - 5 years	**531336.52**

Foreclosure Costs to Lender

Current Value of Property	420000.00
Maximum "Fast Sale" Value	378000.00
Additional Holding costs	15000.00
Foreclosure Expenses	5000.00
Selling Expenses	26460.00
Possible Recovery - Foreclosure	336540.00
Cost to 1st Lender	**281088.50**

1st Loan Past Due Interest	0.00	75000.00
Deferred Interest	0.00	0.00
Total Balance	442159.62	566000.00
P&I Payment - 1st	2867.84	2867.84
New Interest Rate - 1st	6.750%	4.500%
Number of Months	360	360
Taxes and Insurance	462.50	462.50
Total Payments	3330.34	3330.34
Loss in Principle to 1st Lender	48840.38	0.00
Loss in Deferred Interest to 1st Lender	75000.00	0.00
Interest Paid to 1st Lender	144991.19	122024.14
Loan Balance after 5 Years	415080.48	515953.81
Interest lost due to foreclosure	16483.63	51628.50
Income to 1st Lender 5 Years after Modification	-79667.18	173652.64

These proposals were made at a time when interest rates were still around 5 – 5.5%. This was a Countrywide/Bank of America loan and at about the time that the California Attorney General's office, under now governor Jerry Brown, filed suit against Countrywide for their predatory and misleading lending programs. In October of 2008, Bank of America, on behalf of Countrywide, executed a stipulated judgment whereby they agreed to modify certain types of loans without the lengthy paperwork requirement that the bank had demanded in the past. The modifications were to be based upon the borrower's present verifiable income, and the process was to take no more than 60 days.

The loan in these charts was the type that the Bank of America had agreed to modify without the red tape. When I confronted the Robo-Answerer (what they comically referred to as their "Home Retention Team") with the terms of this Stipulated Judgment, they claimed to know nothing of it and had to do what they were instructed. They never looked at my documentation and consistently required that something new had to be submitted to them, even though my office had previously submitted the same documents.

The frustrating part was that there was never a single point of contact, even though one was required by Federal Law when the borrower had requested certain information be provided to them. We would call the Home Retention Team and be required to punch in the loan number and social security number of the borrower, and then confess to the fact that it was not the borrower calling but a 3rd party. When speaking to someone there, I would get the same answers each and every time. "We are waiting for the file to be assigned to a negotiator" or "It is with the negotiator and we are waiting for a response from the investor" or "These things take time, and you should check back in 30 days". They never called you first.

After four months of negotiating with them, the bank refused to modify the loan and threatened to go forward with the foreclosure. Remember, my client has not made a payment on this loan for almost 18 months! We tried a new tactic ... I filed a lawsuit in January, 2009 against Bank of America and

Countrywide claiming various causes of action seeking a temporary restraining order and injunction to block the foreclosure sale.

When I did that, the matter was assigned to an outside attorney to represent Bank of America. He agreed that it made more sense to attempt to reach a modification of the loan rather than spend the money on litigation. He got in contact with Bank of America, and the case was continued a couple of times in the hopes that the matter could be settled in a reasonable manner. On April 16th I received a letter of modification and settlement from Bank of America (not the attorney). There were two problems with it that made it impossible to agree to. The first was that it had to be returned to BofA no later than April 5, 2009 (11 days before I received it) and it released Bank of America of any further liability to my client. We couldn't do the first, and wouldn't do the second.

After discussing the matter with the other attorney, I received another letter from Bank of America near the end of May giving my client until June 10, 2009 to reply with an acceptance. They had eliminated the release of liability, but the terms of the modification were more that of a forbearance. They reduced the payments to a level that I had requested for 4 months, and then showed that on the fifth month the entire past due was due. There was nothing that stated that if they maintained these trial payments for a period of time, they would modify the note permanently or for a more extended period of time.

In the mean time the market had continued to plummet and the property was now well under $400,000 and dropping. I finally met with my clients to discuss the matter with them and that is when I coined the phrase, which I later passed on to the judge, that "you can't fight stupid." I explained that they were going to incur more and more attorney fees fighting something that they may never win, and that they would be better off just dismissing the lawsuit, keep saving their money and stay as long as the could. It would take them at least five years to recover the loss in market value in comparison with the loan. They agreed, and we dismissed the lawsuit without prejudice.

The interesting thing is that after the lawsuit was dismissed, the client continued to live in the house and the lender contacted them regarding a mortgage modification. After living in the house for 38 months without making a payment, the bank modified the loan by shaving $100,000 off the principle and reducing the interest rate to 2.85%. I am not sure I even want to understand the logic of the lenders and servicers in this matter.

This is not to say that there were not some successes. After working these for awhile, I learned that in some cases there was a great deal of flexibility in the agreement for the management of the trusts that had the mortgages and the servicers, while in others the servicers were not given such latitude.

I had one client whose loan was modified to 2.75% for the life of the loan and the term extended to 38 years, amortized. Her payments were reduced by 70% and she was able to retain ownership of her home. I know of another individual who was actually contacted by the lender and offered a reduction without even asking for it. They were a smaller portfolio lender, meaning that the group who made the loan still had the loan, and they understood the benefit of receiving something rather than getting a house back that they would be required to sell.

Unfortunately, I have had clients who had received a very reasonable modification offer, but because of job losses or reduction in income, were unable to even make those payments.

I have often heard or read statements from the big lenders saying that the majority of the loans that were modified ended up being in default again, and having the foreclosure process start up once more. That is partially accurate and partially inaccurate. Many of the "modifications" that they talked about were actually forbearance agreements. That means that the loans were not actually modified, but that the past due balances were put into the loan for payment later, and occasionally they reduced the interest rate on the loan by one-half on a percent.

In other cases, they put someone on a three month "trial" payment plan while they reviewed the modification package. One client came to me because he had been paying what turned out to me one of these trial payment plans, which was $1,000 per month less than the actual loan, for a year! When I reviewed the original letter that he had received, it stated "Congratulations! It *appears* that you *might* qualify for a modification in the terms of your loan." I added the emphasis and the underlining for the reader, but it was not marked that way in the actual letter.

After making these payments for a full year, he received a phone call informing him that, after review of the file, the investor was not willing to modify the promissory note, and that he would be required to repay the $12,000.00 difference from the reduced payment within 30 days, or they would begin foreclosure proceedings.

Of course, the scammers got involved in mortgage modifications, including many attorneys.

Real estate agents or mortgage brokers were not allowed to take advanced payments, so they would get together with an attorney who would draft and engagement letter, and would collect a retainer or a set fee. The attorney would then turn the file over to the agents to do the negotiating, keep part of the fee for himself and pass the rest to the agents. Most of those attorneys did nothing with the file to help the homeowner.

I worked with about twelve clients with sixteen properties in an effort to help them keep their homes. I made the vast majority of the phone calls myself, and eventually learned that the fact that I was an attorney meant nothing to the person taking the call on the other end. They were required to stick to their script, and were never able to transfer you to a supervisor. It is my belief that if you were transferred to a so-called supervisor, you actually ended up talking to the clown at the next desk.

My frustration reached new heights when in November of 2008 I was on the phone with Wells Fargo trying to stop a foreclosure scheduled for 2 days after the date I was making the phone call. I was on the phone for more than three hours, being transferred from one person and department to then next. I was threatening a lawsuit if they did not postpone the foreclosure sale until the mortgage modification package was reviewed and acted upon. I finally got transferred to someone in the office of the foreclosure trustee, who asked me to hold on for a minute. When he came back, he said "This is a Fannie Mae loan, and all Fannie Mae foreclosures had been postponed until January."

It was then that I realized that the people who had been hired to do the modification jobs were totally incompetent and that the entire modification process would be doomed for failure. For the most part, my prediction has come true.

The government provided various incentives and programs to entice lenders and servicers to modify mortgages rather than forecloses. Unfortunately, they put the loan servicing companies in charge of implementing and managing the programs set up by the government. The servicers would take six months or more to process the paperwork, negotiate with the investor, seek new sets of the same documents that had been delivered to them just the month before, and drag out the process.

There is a simple reason that they took so much time to work the process. The servicing companies had contracts with the lender/investor to service the loan for a monthly fee based upon the value of the loan. They discouraged a reduction in principle because that would reduce the fee they received. They, in many cases, discouraged modifications because if the loan was foreclosed, they would be paid the full amount owed to them upon sale of the property. They could create and manage their own cash flow.

Giving the servicers control of managing the program was about the same as putting the wolf in charge of guarding a flock of sheep. Someone was going to have a nice lunch today.

In a later chapter, I will discuss my thoughts as to how the collapse and the severity of it could have been prevented or at least minimized.

Chapter 8

The National and Global Disaster

America's mortgage backed securities had now poisoned the world. As early as September of 2007 the Bank of China revealed that they had suffered from subprime investment losses. The British bank Northern Rock faced a run on the bank by depositors until the British government stepped in to guarantee all of the savings accounts. In December, the European Central Bank had to extend loans to many commercial banks on the verge of default. In February, 2008 Deutsche Bank and Commerzbank in Germany had to take severe write-downs in the value of their portfolios.

Many banks in Europe invested in or provided to their customers investments in mortgage backed securities, many of them for subprime loans.

In the United States dozens of large retail outlets have either entirely closed their door or closed thousands of locations. Circuit City filed for bankruptcy in 2008. Levitz Furniture, a store that goes back to 1910, closed all of its locations. Mervyn's department stores closed nationwide.

The automobile industry was on the verge of collapse, losing billions of dollars each year. General Motors, under a government sponsored plan, filed for Chapter 11 Bankruptcy as the United States Government purchased shares of its stock, and therefore became part owner of a company that could not survive on its own. Even Toyota, which was now the largest automobile manufacturer in the world, lost money during this time; something that it had never previously experienced. Thousands of people lost their jobs and many companies that supported the automobile industry went out of business. The New United Motor Manufacturing, Inc. (NUMMI) shut down in Fremont, California after GM terminated its partnership agreement with Toyota, and Toyota decided not to go forward on its own.

How did these giant companies become so affected? It goes back to the artificial prosperity that the country was enjoying based on the inflation of home prices and people taking advantage of the easy credit available to them through Home Equity Lines of Credit to buy the bigger truck or SUV. As the housing industry prospered, the entire economy prospered.

I thought that with so many foreclosures, the cost of rent would go up dramatically. The opposite occurred. People lost their homes because they had lost their jobs and now had a negative credit report. They couldn't even afford the rent, so they moved in with family members or shared a place with other people. Now investors had property that sat empty. Rents dropped. Sometimes, people would rent a house only to learn that the owner had not been making mortgage payments and that a lender was preparing to foreclose. The owner of the house would file bankruptcy, and in many cases the renter lost his deposit and was evicted by the lender.

Suddenly, Americans could not buy things at the rate they had in the past. Inventories at retailers in the United States soared, and therefore their orders from manufacturers stopped. Manufacturers throughout the world, including China, Korea, Japan, Europe and elsewhere began experiencing a stockpile of inventory of their own. Soon workers in China were going back to the farms with their families.

As fewer people bought or were able to buy things that had kept the economy flowing, the ripple effect led to more business failures. Following is a partial list of major business failures in 2008 and 2009. Some of these companies continued to operate under Bankruptcy protection, while others closed their doors permanently.

(See chart on the next page)

2008

☐ Aloha Airlines	☐ Photo-Optix
☐ ATA Airlines	☐ Pilgrim's Pride
☐ Bennigan's	☐ Sharper Image
☐ Buffets, Inc.	☐ Shoe Pavilion
☐ Circuit City	☐ Tribune Company
☐ Countrywide Financial	☐ Tropicana Resort & Casino
☐ Frontier Airlines	☐ Value City
☐ IndyMac Bank	☐ VeraSun Energy
☐ Lehman Brothers	☐ Vivitar
☐ Lenox	☐ Wachovia
☐ Levitz Furniture	☐ Washington Mutual
☐ Lillian Vernon	☐ Wickes Furniture
☐ Linens 'n Things	☐ Wilsons Leather
☐ Madoff Investment Securities	☐ WiQuest Communications
☐ Mattress Discounters	☐ Woolworths Group
☐ Mervyns	☐ XL Airways UK
☐ Nationwide Airlines	☐ Yamato Life Insurance Company
☐ Olan Mills	☐ Zoom Airlines

☐ Allied Carpets	☐ Nortel Networks
☐ Borders UK	☐ Peanut Corporation of America
☐ CIT Group	
☐ Boater's World	☐ Philadelphia Media Holdings
☐ Colonial Bancgroup	
☐ Central Park Media	☐ The Reader's Digest Association
☐ Charter Communications	
	☐ Ritz Camera
☐ Extended Stay Hotels	☐ Silicon Graphics
	☐ Steve & Barry's
☐ Fleetwood Enterprises	☐ Sun-Times Media Group
☐ Gottschalks	☐ Taylor, Bean & Whitaker
☐ KB Toys	
☐ Land of Leather	☐ Trump Entertainment Resorts
☐ Monaco Coach Corporation	
	☐ Viyella
	☐ Waterford Wedgwood
	☐ Young Broadcasting

This list does not include many of the companies which were bailed out by the Federal Government, such as Bank of America, General Motors and AIG. Nor does it include the thousands of small to large companies that simply closed their doors or laid of hundreds of thousands of employees in an attempt to remain in business. Profitability was no longer the goal for these companies; surviving was all they cared about.

You will also notice that Fannie Mae and Freddie Mac are not on the lists. Those entities which had been independent and

It goes on and on … everyone in the world is tied to someone else in one way or another.

Greece, Ireland, Spain, and many other countries have had to be helped by those that had stronger economies. The economy of the entire world, which had so depended upon the glutinous consumption of Americans, no longer had the free and easy spending American consumer to purchase their products. The world had relied on our consumers for so many years and didn't have sources for their products.

Toyota, for example, had thousand of vehicles sitting in lots at their American assembly plants and at the seaports. There was no need to build any more cars or trucks, of the parts that went into them.

As construction died in America, so did the need for raw materials, appliances, tools, work clothes, or anything else needed by the construction industry.

Could anything have been done to avoid this disaster, or at least lessen the effect it has had on the world? We will explore that in the next chapter.

Chapter 9

How the Collapse Could Have Been Prevented

This disaster could have been avoided entirely, or at least brought under control before it got out of hand. Hindsight is always 20/20, so we can see the mistakes that were made. Unfortunately, we cannot buy a ticket back in time to 1980 to change the things that took place since then.

I have discussed the deregulations that took place in the 1980's and 1990's that gave banks and Wall Street so much leeway. Alan Greenspan was a huge promoter of the free market system and that less government regulation was better than more. He was named as the Chairman of the Federal Reserve Bank in 1987 by then president, Ronald Reagan. President Bill Clinton reappointed him to that position later in his presidency.

President Clinton also appointed Robert Rubin, who served from January 20, 1993, to January 10, 1995, in the White House as Assistant to the President for Economic Policy. In that capacity, he directed the National Economic Council, which Bill Clinton created after winning the presidency. On January 11, 1995, Rubin was named as the United States Secretary of Treasury, where he served until July 2, 1999. Prior to joining the Clinton Administration, Rubin spent 26 years at Goldman Sachs eventually serving as a member of the Board, and Co-Chairman from 1990-1992.

Another addition to the Clinton administration was Larry Summers. In 1993 Summers was appointed Undersecretary for International Affairs and later in the United States Department of the Treasury under the Clinton Administration. In 1995, he was promoted to Deputy Secretary of the Treasury under his long-time political mentor Robert Rubin. In 1999, he succeeded Rubin as Secretary of the Treasury.

Summers hailed the Gramm-Leach-Bliley Act in 1999, which lifted more than six decades of restrictions against banks offering commercial banking, insurance, and investment services (by repealing key provisions in the 1933 Glass-Steagall Act): "Today Congress voted to update the rules that have governed financial services since the Great Depression and replace them with a system for the 21st century," Summers said. "This historic legislation will better enable American companies to compete in the new economy." Many critics, including President Barack Obama, have suggested the 2007 subprime mortgage financial crisis was caused by the partial repeal of the 1933 Glass-Steagall Act. Indeed, as a member of President Clinton's Working Group on Financial Markets, Summers, along with U.S. Securities and Exchange Commission (SEC) Chairman Arthur Levitt, Fed Chairman Greenspan, and Secretary Rubin, torpedoed an effort to regulate the derivatives that many blame for bringing the financial market down in Fall 2008.

With the boom in the economy at that time, who could have possibly have wanted to strengthen the regulations on any part of Wall Street, which was leading the country in the economic successes at the time.

The person who attempted to warn of the dangers of an unregulated Over the Counter (OTC) Derivative market was a woman by the name of Brooklsey Born. She had been considered by Clinton as a possible Attorney General, but he found her to be "boring." However, she had become friendly with Hillary Clinton through their association in the legal profession, and he subsequently named her as the Chairperson for the Commodity Futures Trading Commission (CFTC). This was a little known regulatory commission which regulated Agriculture Futures and other commodity futures. It also had the duty to regulate the OTC Derivative market.

In 1995, Proctor and Gamble and other corporate clients sued Bankers Trust over the sale of derivative products to those companies. These corporations alleged that Bankers Trust had sold them products that were so complex that even their own internal experts could not understand them, and ultimately, the corporations lost millions of dollars through those purchases. This law suit caught the attention of Born, and she began looking into the possibility of establishing regulations to control this hidden market. Born was very concerned about swaps, financial instruments that are traded over the counter between banks, insurance companies or other funds or companies, and thus have no transparency except to the two counterparties and the counterparties' regulators.

On May 7, 1998, the CFTC issued a Concept Release soliciting input from regulators, academics, and practitioners to determine "how best to maintain adequate regulatory safeguards without impairing the ability of the OTC (Over-the-counter) derivatives market to grow and the ability of U.S. entities to remain competitive in the global financial marketplace." Unfortunately, Greenspan, Rubin and Summers were all of the same mindset – regulation is bad for the economy, and the market will take care of itself, including the regulation of potentially fraudulent activity.

On July 30, 1998, then-Deputy Secretary of the Treasury Summers testified before congress that "the parties to these kinds of contract are largely sophisticated financial institutions that would appear to be eminently capable of protecting themselves from fraud and counterparty insolvencies." Summers, like Greenspan and Rubin who also opposed the concept release, offered no proof that the contracts would not be misused by financial institutions. Summers testified that "to date there has been no clear evidence of a need for additional regulation of the institutional OTC derivatives market, and we would submit that proponents of such regulation must bear the burden of demonstrating that need." This argument suggests that the default position in the disagreement was that Summers, Greenspan, and Rubin were right, and that anyone (i.e., Brooksley Born) who disagreed with them bore the burden of proving their position.

The lack of regulation that allowed A.I.G. to sell hundreds of billions of dollars in credit default swaps on mortgage-backed securities was a direct result of efforts by the Treasury (first under Rubin and then under Summers), the Federal Reserve (under Greenspan), and the Securities and Exchange Commission (under Arthur Levitt) to deregulate the derivatives markets. The first response to the CFTC Concept Release was issued as a joint statement from Rubin, Greenspan, and Levitt who stated that they "have grave concerns about this action and its possible consequences." These four people convinced Congress, which viewed them as God's gift to the great economy, to dismiss Born's ideas of regulating the Derivative market.

Brooksley Born's prediction came true when in 1998, a hedge fund by the name of Long Term Capital Management, which was making showing profits in the billions of dollars through the OTC Derivative market, collapsed under its own house of cards. Fifteen banks worldwide had to infuse more than $3.6 billion in order to avoid a financial crisis, which would have been a further warning that there was a need to regulate this market. Some experts said that Federal Reserve Bank of New York involvement in the rescue, however small, would encourage large financial institutions to assume more risk, in the belief that the Federal Reserve would intervene on their behalf in the event of trouble.

Of course, as we all know, the derivative market continued to thrive with the mortgage backed securities and credit default swaps that helped feed the frenzy of investors at the top and the bottom of the investment chain, as well as potential homeowners who where just looking for a home to live in.

Levitt and Greenspan have admitted that their views on this issue were wrong. Levitt told WGBH in Boston that "I could have done much better. I could have made a difference." Greenspan told a congressional hearing that "I found a flaw ... in the model that I perceived is the critical functioning structure that defines how the world works." When Summers was asked about the financial crisis in an ABC interview on March 15, 2009, Summers replied that "there are a lot of terrible things that have happened in the last eighteen months, but what's happened at A.I.G. ... the way it was not regulated, the way no one was watching ... is outrageous." This statement was made after he had fought deregulation, and basically stripped, with the help of Greenspan, Levitt and Rubin, any authority that Brooksley Born had.

So much for what could have been done prior to the collapse of the housing market; what could have been done to lessen the severity of the collapse after it was apparent that the volume of sub-prime loans, along with home loans with no equity, was going to further erode prices. After all, the economic experts in the government and at all of the major lending institutions were well educated with degrees at such places as Harvard, Yale, MIT, etc. The one thing they all had was an allegiance to the companies that the worked for or supported the political parties or affiliations that they had. What they lacked was some common sense and a true understanding of the real estate market and how much it meant to the country.

The "Troubled (Toxic) Asset Relief Program" was established to bail out the banking (Goldman Sachs, Bank of America, etc.) and insurance industry (AIG) from the situation that they had created through their unique lending and OTC Derivative practices. These companies made billions of dollars over the years through these transactions, which was spent on higher salaries and bonuses for those who could best manipulate the market. The United States Treasury, also known as you and me, provided $800 billion to bail them out. Did they use those funds to stabilize the housing market, which had benefited them so well during the boom years?

The answer is a simple "No." Instead, they invested those funds in other markets which would provide them with fast profits which would enable them to pay back the government more quickly. They had to do that because the government, now having a vested interest in the businesses, was able to control the amount of salaries and bonuses that would be paid to the executives. The faster they could get the government out of their hair, the faster they could re-establish their bonus structure and the lifestyle they had become accustomed to.

Where else could this money have gone that would have helped to stabilize the housing market, and therefore the entire economy? I had a plan in late 2007 and in 2008 which would have done just that. The first idea was one of those ideas would not have cost a single dollar to the government or the taxpayers. It would have been to temporarily require the elimination of the "Due on Sale" clause from all promissory notes and deeds of trust for existing loans. This would have given homeowners who knew that they would not be able to obtain re-financing when an adjustable rate was triggered to sell their property to someone who could have afforded the payments, or had the financial strength to pay down a significant amount and refinance the property at a lower amount and interest rate.

The second idea was to use that $800 billion and buy down the interest rate on every loan in

America to a more affordable amount, say 4.5% - 5%. There are approximately 48 million homes in the United States that had mortgages. Many of these mortgages had a significant amount of equity, while others had zero equity. Some also had good fixed rates, while others had negative amortized loans, a form of an adjustable loan, or some other sub-prime loan product. Now, if we look at that $800 billion number and divided it by 48 million homes, there would have approximately $17,000.00 available, on average, to buy down the interest rate and convert it to a fixed loan for 5-7 years.

I have heard all of the arguments from people at the time I made that suggestion. That wouldn't be fair to those who were more careful in their purchase or put more money down, or that they did not want to help pay for those who were not deserving of owning a house anyway.

The reality is that those people, who did not want to help those who had been taken advantage of or got caught in the lenders' predatory lending scheme, have suffered just as much with their lost equity and, in many cases, lost jobs. Let's take a look at an analysis of who really lost when the prices started dropping and no one wanted to "bail-out" the buyers who made bad decisions. The scenario is that two people bought identical homes in the same neighborhood at a price of $500,000.00. Buyer A, whose credit was marginal and could only get a sub-prime loan, put nothing down and had 2 mortgages; one for 80% of the price and one for the remaining 20% of the price. Buyer B, whose credit was excellent and was able to make a 20% down payment, had only one mortgage at 80% loan to value.

The chart on the next page demonstrates that those who didn't want to "bail out" the irresponsible homebuyers were the ones who were hurt the most. By resisting the help to those who were irresponsible, they took their own equity and threw it away without even realizing it.

	Buyer A	Buyer B
Purchase Price - 2006	500000.00	$500000.00
Down Payment	0.00	$100000.00
1st Loan Interest Rate Payment	400,000.00 2.9% pmt, 6.5% actual $1,664.92	$400,000.00 5.5% fixed $2,271.16
2nd Loan Interest Rate Payment	100,000.00 6.5%, Interest only $541.67	None
Present Value	$375000.00	$375000.00
Out of Pocket Loss	Nothing	$100000.00

The big loser is the guy who was responsible, and put down 20% and had a fixed loan. He, in most cases, was the one who was most vocal against those who had been irresponsible, and took on more than they could handle or didn't pay attention to the terms of what he was signing. The lenders took Buyer B's $100,000.00 down payment; while the irresponsible Buyer B only lost the place that he was living in on the lender's investment.

How would my second plan have worked, and how would it have benefited the troubled banking system? Let's take one house and one mortgage, as an example. The house was purchased at the peak for $600,000 and has a loan for the same amount. It is a negative amortized loan, meaning that the homeowner is paying less each month than what is due under the fully amortized rate of, let's say, 6.5%. The payments on such a fully amortized loan (we will assume one loan, although there would have been two loans) would be $3,792.41 per month, but they were only paying $2,497.38 (2.9% teaser rate). Now, if the government was to have paid 3% of the loan amounts to buy down the interest rate to a fixed for 5-7 years, the payments on that same mortgage, fixed at 4.5%, would be $3,040.11. It would have been a much easier step to pay $542.00 more per month than almost $1,300.00 more per month.

This would not have been a gift to these homeowners, either. Whatever was paid to buy down the loan would be added to the balance of the mortgage and recovered when the property sold or was refinanced.

Would this program kept values from going down? Probably not, because as we have already discussed, the real estate values were much higher than they realistically should have been. However, it would have helped to reduce the reduction in values. We have already seen how the wholesale level of foreclosures drove down the prices to a level where others simply walked away, realizing that it would take ten years for the market to come back.

Would this program eliminated foreclosures? Of course not, because there were those who could not have made higher payments even if the interest rate and payments were brought down to a lower level. There still would have been industries that lost jobs, which would have led to people who could not make payments at any rate. The point is that fewer people would have defaulted, because the payments would never have adjusted to the higher level.

We have all heard about the "Trickle Down" theory, where money is delivered in bulk to the top of the pyramid and it would trickle down to the masses. You have seen it before, but take a look at the figure on the next page to get an idea of the concept. The truth is that the money usually does not, and certainly did not in this crisis, trickle down to where it benefited the homeowners.

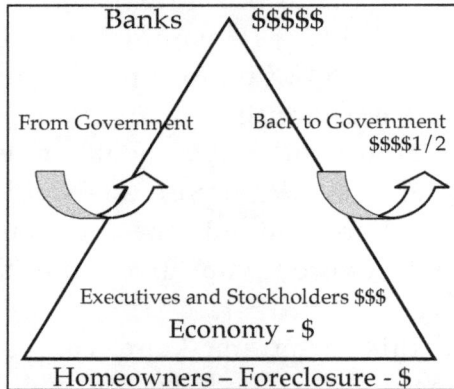

The truth of the matter is that the trickle-down theory does work, provided that you turn the pyramid upside down first. If that $800 billion had been delivered to the homeowners in the form of mortgage reductions, the banks would not have reached the stage where they would have needed to be bailed out! Why? Because the loans would not have become "Troubled (Toxic) Assets" – they would have been a good portfolio that was simply not generating the type of profits that they had hoped for. The following figure is my pyramid:

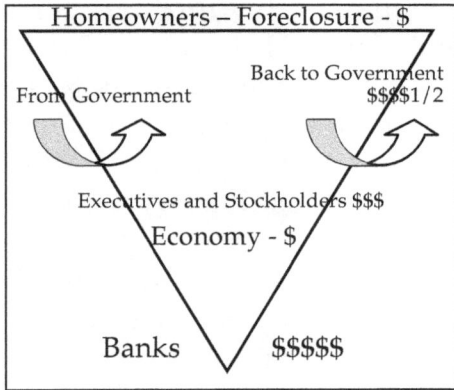

Unfortunately, the government went along with their plan and bailed out the banks and the investment banks, because they were too big to fail, and they feared a total collapse of the financial sector. The truth is that the real estate and housing market was too big to fail, but fail it did because the government could not see how important it was to the overall economy.

The amount of employment that was lost with the collapse of the housing market is staggering. The worst area affected was construction, as developers ceased building because there was already a glut of homes on the market. So many jobs that are linked to the housing and construction business are overlooked. They include architects, title and escrow personnel, loan processors, inspection companies, surveyors, lumber processors, appliance and other hardware manufacturers and suppliers, flooring companies, real estate agents, property managers, and more. It will be many years before these businesses recover from this calamity.

Once the extent of the collapse became apparent, the government, State and Federal, tried numerous techniques to forestall foreclosures and create demand for real estate. California added a requirement that the lender discuss loan modifications prior to going forward with a foreclosure. All that really did was add a few months to someone living in the property without making payments before the bank foreclosed.

There were Federal and, in California, tax credits for first time homebuyers, and then for Buyers who had recently sold a home. Those created a little stimulation, and helped to level off the inventory for a brief time. Those incentives ended, and prices again started to drop and foreclosures crept higher again.

We have all read about the "Robo-Signers" who would sign documents that they had not even read in order to process foreclosures more quickly. Lawsuits have been filed by many people who lost their homes in foreclosure, claiming that the process was not handled correctly. Some title companies have refused to provide title insurance to buyers of foreclosed homes because of the possibility of a previous owner filing a claim against a new buyer and the lender claiming that they still own the home. The title company would be required to defend the buyer of the property against the previous owner.

I mentioned in the chapter regarding mortgage modifications about the incentives that the government tried to give lenders and servicers in order to reduce the number of foreclosures and increase the number who have the ability to remain in their homes. These measures, too, have failed miserably. The fact is that investors still have no faith in the housing market and would rather pull their money, take their losses (with the associated tax benefits) and invest what is left in something that they believe will give them a return.

This chapter was about how the collapse could have been prevented, which is now water under the bridge. In the next chapter, I will discuss the future of real estate prices.

Chapter 10

Will There Be Another Real Estate Boom?

Everyone wants to know if the market will ever come back. There is a simple answer to that question: YES! The real question that needs to be asked is how soon and how quickly will they come back. That is a tougher question to answer. Once again, we must look back to where we were in order to determine where we are going.

I once heard that the value of real estate would rise at the inflation rate plus two times the rate of population increase. In other words, if the value of real estate was $100,000 in January of a given year, the inflation (I) rate was 2.5% and the population (P) grew at 3%; the value of real estate at the end of the year would be 8.5% higher, or $108,500.

$100,000 x (I + 2P) = $108,500

I decided to put that theory to a test, starting with the actual median price home in California in 1968, when it was $23,210. I ran a spread sheet using

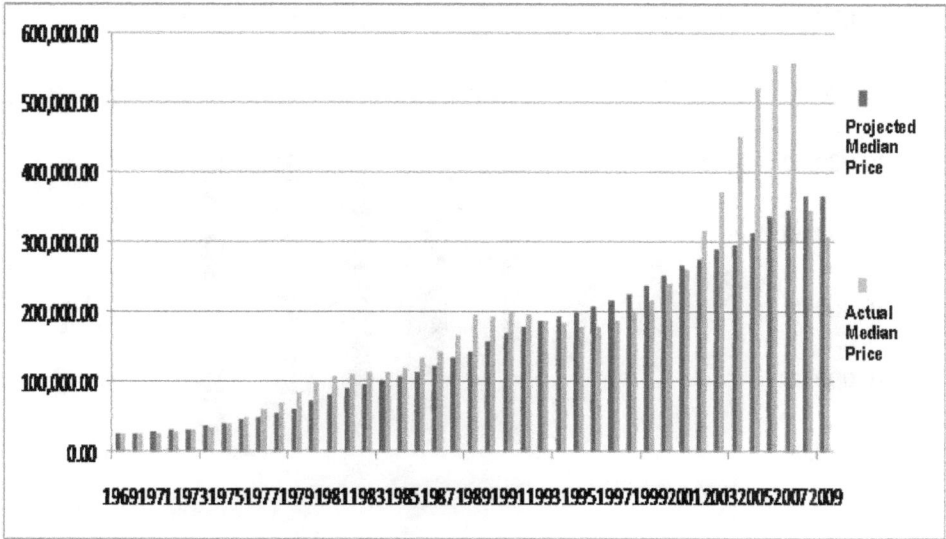

On the other hand, when I used the formula that called for using inflation plus two times the population growth, I came up with $529,600 for the median price in California at the end of 2009, compared to the actual median price of $306,820. Obviously, the factor of population growth had to be somewhere in between. What I found came the closest was multiply the median price at the beginning of the year (M1) by the sum of the rate of inflation (I) plus 1.4 times the rate of population growth (P) to get the projected median price at the end of the year (M2). The charts that I refer to in the remainder of this chapter will be based on that formula, shown as follows: M1 x (I + 1.4P) = M2. The following chart shows the projected median prices base on the formula, compared to the actual pricing. We will go over certain time periods in more detail throughout this chapter.

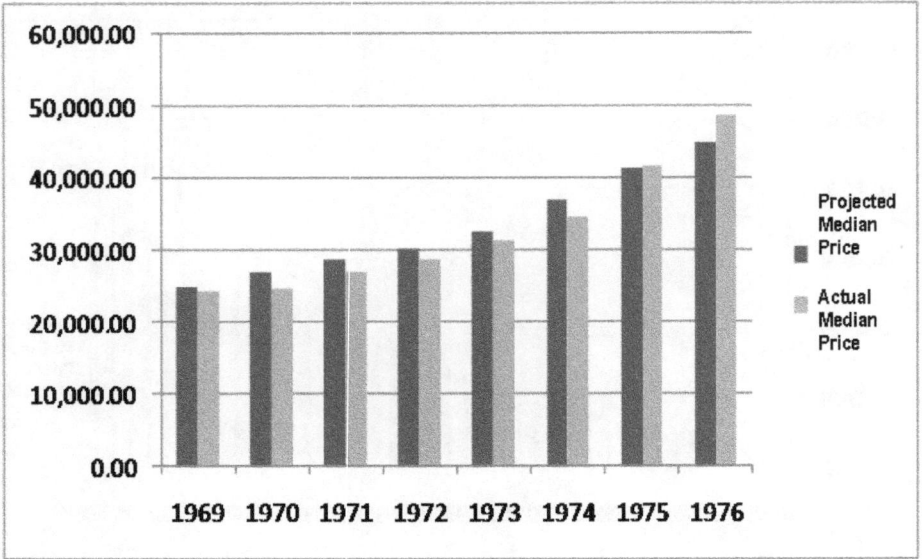

Legend:
- Projected Median Price
- Actual Median Price

to the accuracy of the market, and was within less than 10% of the actual market, and in most years within 5%. To be precise, the actual median price was slightly lower than that of the formula until 1976.

The next chart shows how closely the actual pricing followed the formula.

In 1977, Jimmy Carter took office as President of the United States after his defeat of President Gerald Ford, who had succeeded Richard Nixon. The voters were probably still concerned by Ford's association with Nixon and the Watergate scandal, as well as his terrible golf swing. The country entered a period of uncontrolled, double digit inflation, with the prime interest rate that peaked at over 20% in 1981. Even with these high interest rates, real estate values continued to soar, with the actual median price exceeding the formula price by as much as 27% in some years.

As you can see from the following chart, the prices were substantially higher than the projected median price.

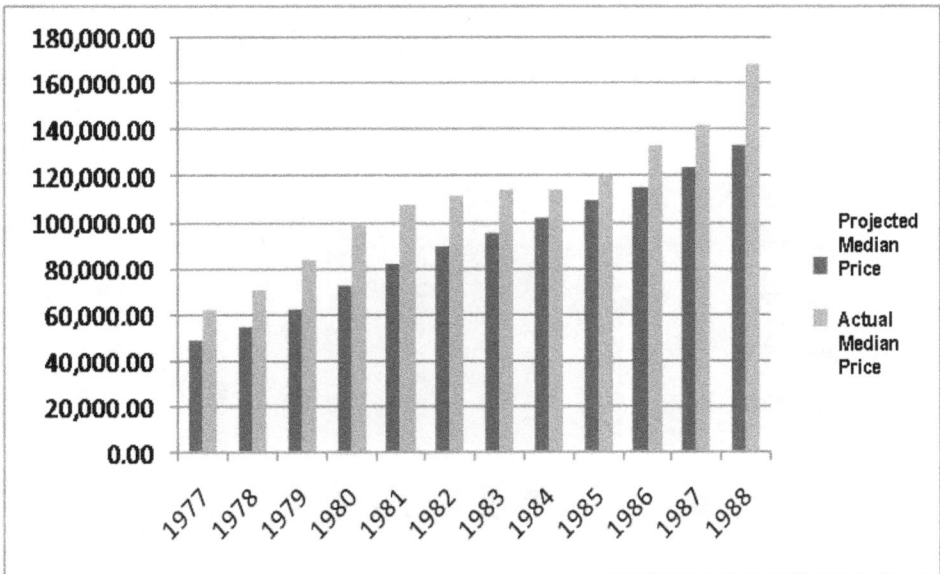

high. But remember what I said in the beginning of

the book about how people circumvented those interest rates by assuming low interest first loans, and either obtaining new institutional second mortgages or seller carry-back mortgages, which enabled the seller to sell his property at interest rates that averaged out to be below the market rate. In just 15 years, median price of homes jumped from $48,630 at the end of 1976 to $200,660, an increase of $152,030, or over 312%. That is an average of almost 21% per year.

That rate slowed down, and there was actually a drop in the median price over between 1992 through 1996, when the median price home fell from its high of $200,660 to $177,270, a drop of about 12% over that time period.

In 1993, the median price projection formula amount of $186,485 was almost exactly equal to the 1993 median price of $188,240, less than 1% difference. As you can see by the chart, although the prices went down, they subsequently recovered and began climbing again.

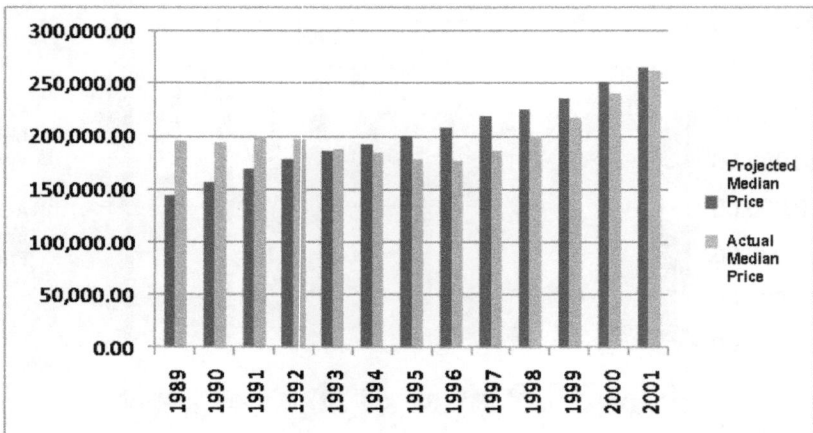

In 2002, the boom began with easy credit, mortgage backed securities and sub-prime loans.

There was a seemingly endless supply of money for mortgages and seemingly an endless supply of people wanting to purchase residential real estate, either for a home or an investment. As prices went up, a feeding frenzy occurred where there would be 30 offers or more on a house, and each time the price was driven higher. Appraisers could not keep up with the rapid increase, and had nothing to rely on except the fact that the properties were in demand, and the buyer was setting the fair market price.

Of course, the only way that anyone could afford these properties was for the money market to continue to have a supply of easy money with payment rates lower than what the actual interest rates were. Since, that did not happen, the market collapsed and the rest is history. The following chart shows the dramatic increase of prices, created by the "Liar Loan" products which provided an artificial appearance of prosperity, followed by the dramatic crash.

The charts that I prepared used the formula on an ongoing basis using the actual median price in

1968 and then multiplying the formula against the projected median price, even if it was much greater or lower than the actual median price of homes. I have included the chart of those numbers in Appendix A. If I took that same formula and multiplied by the actual median price at the end of each year, a completely new result occurs. The actual numbers can be found in Appendix B, and the comparable charts using this method, look at Appendix C.

There were only 7 years out of forty where the difference exceeded 10%. One was in 1977 and another in 1990. The other five were in 2002, 2003, and 2004 (in which the actual median price was higher than the formula) and 2008 and 2009 (in which the actual median was lower than the formula.

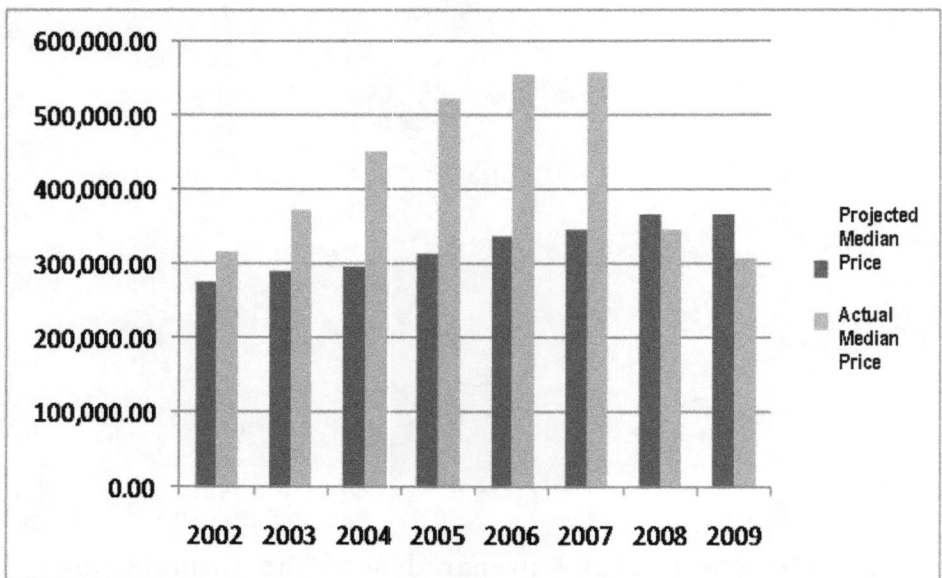

That brings us to what will happen in the future. The following graphs reflect the median prices of real estate in California over the past forty years as well as the formula that I have been discussing in this chapter. The first graph shows the formula used starting with the actual median price in 1968, and then ignoring the actual median prices after that date and multiplying the factor against the projected median price each year.

I am showing the full chart from 1968 to 2009 once more below. The dark column, which represents the formula projection on all the charts, shows a steady growth, year after year. The lighter column, on the other hand, which represents the actual median

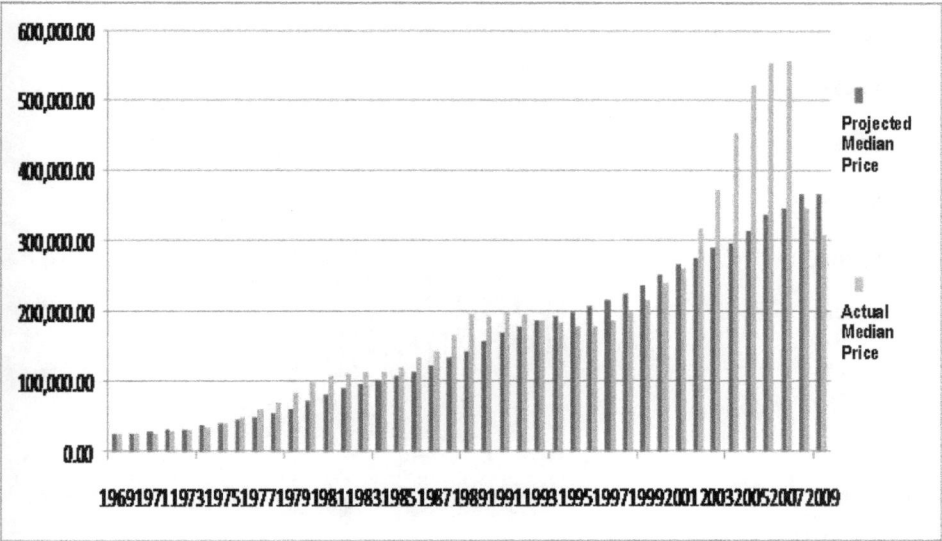

price in California, shows the peaks and valleys of the real estate market. I found it to be most interesting to note that the peaks followed the deregulation of the banks and savings & loans, as well as the shoddy lending practices that they engaged in, and were followed immediately by valleys in the real estate market and lengthy recessions. According to this chart, the projected median price is higher than the current median prices of homes in California.

The second graph shows the actual median price of homes and the formula median price when multiplied against the previous years ending actual median price. In this case, the curves flow very closely with each other until 2002, when the wild fluctuations began in earnest. The shocking collapse created a difference of 70% between the formula projection and the actual median price. Such a drop is

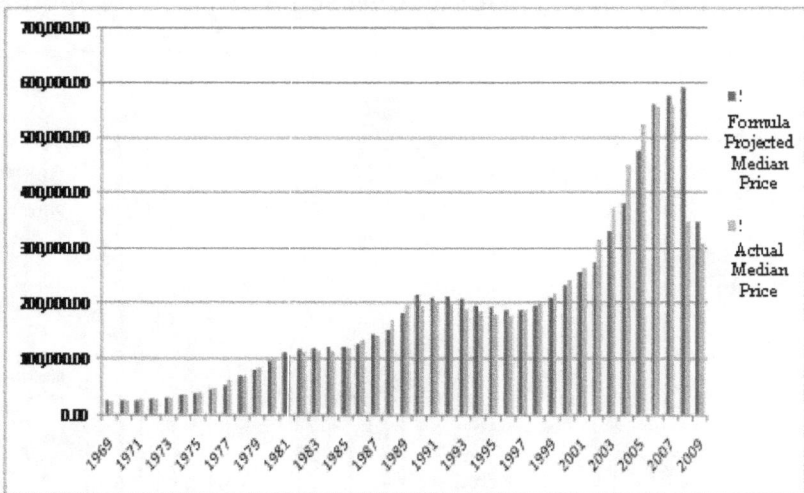

not normal economic sway, but the result of manmade manipulation of the market.

What both of these graphs tell us is that prices in California today are below what either of the formula projects. I am sure that the same would be reflected in most markets. The formula more fairly represents what prices should be reflected in the real estate market, not taking into consideration other influences. Unfortunately, there are other influences that must be considered. They are the availability of financing and the failure of government and business to create sustainable employment. I will discuss that last one in the last chapter, but I do want to touch on the availability of financing here.

As I mentioned earlier in this book, real estate has nothing to do with houses, but everything to do with financing. The boom occurred because of easy financing and lax standards of to whom the loans would be provided. This type of financing artificially drove up the value of houses and provided the country with a false sense of prosperity, which everyone took credit for.

Now, through a knee jerk reaction, the government and banks have completely reversed course and put such stringent controls on lending and home ownership that the market collapsed even further. This was like trying to get a heroin addict to break his habit by giving him a steady flow of Diet Pepsi.

The banks and servicing companies have tried to address the problem that they created with their predatory lending practices by handling the problem as they would have twenty years ago based on more normal loans programs.

Furthermore, the Wall Street boys have tapped out their sources of funds from Mortgage Backed Securities because they are not trusted as being safe, even with the tighter controls placed on the lenders. Then banks are not willing to make loans, either, because they don't want to spend the hard earned that money they were able to generate from their TARP investments.

The bottom line is that, yes, real estate will make a rebound at some point in the future. There will always be a growth in population and there will always be inflation. The lenders will loosen up, because they do not make money unless they loan money. It will take awhile, but I believe that things will stabilize over the next 9 to 30 months, depending on location. Those areas that did not experience the double digit appreciation or severe job losses due to closing of factories or construction jobs will come back sooner, the others later.

Will there be another real estate boom, as there was in the late 1980's and the 2002 – 2006 time period? It is possible, if there is severe inflation in the future, which is quite possible due to the national debt. The other thing to remember is that the government is not very good at learning from its mistakes. There is always the possibility that credit will be loosened up, regulations eased, and investors will need a new place to put their money. Investors are like mothers who have just given birth after nine months of pregnancy. Two hours after giving birth, they have no desire to go through that again. Time, however, erases that memory, and in a couple of years they are pregnant again.

Investors are the same. They will try to make their money anyway that they believe they can. Tax incentives and the prospect of staying ahead of inflation will eventually draw the investors back into the real estate market. That will drive up prices, too, but hopefully not at the pace that has been experienced during the balloon days.

The main thing to remember is that ownership of your primary residence is still the only borrowing investment that should be made. It should be done with the idea that the equity that builds up will remain with the property, and not be taken out to support a lifestyle that one cannot otherwise afford. The tax incentives and the hedge against inflation make primary residence home ownership a wise investment.

While investing in income producing property, such as single family residences, duplexes and apartments for rental purposes, it must be remembered that these are income producing properties to be held over the long haul, not something that should be purchased with the idea of turning a fast profit due to inflation. I have always told investor clients that they must plan on and have the ability to hold investment property for at least 10 years, and if they do that, they will realize a substantial profit.

There is a saying in the stock market – "Bears make money, Bulls make money, but Pigs get slaughtered." That saying is based on the investors, not the Wall Street wizards who concocted the derivative market. They always make money at the expense of the investors or the taxpayers. My point is that that saying applies to real estate, too. It wasn't the Bears or the Bulls that destroyed the real estate market, and therefore the economy, but the Pigs.

Chapter 11

Lessons for Future Real Estate Investors

This is a very short chapter to give potential real estate investors some simple advice before they get into the investment market.

Many investors are still quite nervous about getting into real estate investments. That is quite understandable, considering the disaster that has occurred in the real estate market and that in many areas, prices continue to drop.

We have all read about the possibility of a double dip in housing prices, and in many areas I believe that it could possibly happen. For about four months in 2010, foreclosures were halted because of serious questions as to whether or not the lenders had followed proper procedures in initiating and completing the foreclosure process.

Law suits were filed by previous owners of homes that the lenders sold after a foreclosure was completed. Some of the sales were overturned, creating issues for the title insurers. Some title insurers refused to issue title policies on foreclosed properties locate in certain states, bringing sales to a screeching halt.

I receive emails almost daily from investment groups having seminars and meetings where they can discuss investment strategies. My fear is that these groups may be leading people who have no business investing in real estate to do so, just as many people who bought houses in 2005-2007 who could not afford them. The difference is that, today, most investors need significant cash to buy such properties.

I also get the "Buy, Fix and Flip" emails, where they will teach you how to invest in distressed real estate, fix them up and sell them for a hefty profit. The problem is that most people will pay more than they should for a distressed property and underestimate how long it will take to rehabilitate the property and how much it will cost.

Those who sponsor these seminars also forget to mention the fact that the income generated is taxable as ordinary income. Many think they can do a tax deferred exchange pursuant to Internal Revenue Code §1031. The fix and flip transactions are not considered to be investments, and those doing them are considered by IRS to be dealers.

As I said in the last chapter, prices of real estate are at their lowest point since 2003 and would appear to be below where they should be. Part of the reason for this is the lack of financing, and those prices could drop even more.

The keys to real estate investment are very simply stated.

1. Don't think of a real estate investment to be a get rich quick deal. Be prepared to hold the

property for a minimum of then years. Real estate investment, and the tax benefits that go with it, are long term investments. Real estate investments were meant to be a long term hedge against inflation. Under normal circumstances and under normal market conditions, that is still an accurate statement. Remember what happens to pigs?

2.   You make your money when you buy the property, not when you sell it. I can see the puzzled look on your face. When there is a feeding frenzy of buying, people will buy anything just to make sure that they do not miss the bandwagon. You must remember that, eventually, you will need to sell that property. If you need to sell the property when the market is slow, it will need to meet the normal requirements of a real estate sale. That is location, price, terms and condition.

You will notice that three of those things can be changed, but one cannot. Unless you want to buy a vacant lot somewhere, pay thousands of dollars to install a new foundation and more to move the house, you will be stuck with the location. If you buy a house in a hot market that backs to a freeway, it will still be backed to a freeway in a slow market. There will also be more competition for potential buyers to choose from. Your only choice will be to change one of those other requirements, which will usually be price. Your anticipated gain could become a huge loss from your portfolio.

3.   Don't bite off more than you can chew. Your first real estate investment should be your primary residence. Don't even think about making a real estate purchase as an investment until you own your own home to live in. Once you own your

primary residence, do not even think about tapping into the equity to purchase an investment property.

I have had numerous consultations with people who had borrowed money against their substantial equity in their primary residences and purchased one or more investment properties in California or, in many cases Arizona, Nevada or Florida. The not only lost all of the investment properties, but their primary residence to foreclosure.

In addition to losing those homes, many were faced with issues such as deficiency judgments and taxes for cancellation of debt.

4. If you are going to invest in real estate, you should set up an LLC to protect you from liability. You should also consider setting up a self directed IRA through which you will buy and sell your real estate investments. That way, your profits will be there in the future when you are no longer working you really need the income.

If you follow those simple keys, you can have a secure future in real estate investment. The important thing is that you must not be greedy, and do not plan to live off the income from your properties.

Remember, real estate investment is long term.

Chapter 12

Conclusion and Final Thoughts

We are still far from a conclusion to this mess the country is in, and estimates are that it could be 3 more years before we see appreciable increases in the job market and stabilization of the housing market. Many state governments are on the verge of bankruptcy, and the Federal government goes deeper in debt every hour. The country is trying to take care, not only of its own residents, but those from the entire world. Herbert Hoover once said, "Blessed are the young, for they shall inherit the national debt."

I once heard Zig Ziglar tell the story of a wise old King who called all of the scholars and wise people of the country to his palace to give them a task. The task was to search the world over for all of the knowledge of mankind, the wisdom of the ages, and put that information into a written form that all could benefit from.

This group went out and learned all there was to know and put it into a written form, and delivered it to the King. There were 28 volumes of books, each about 3 inches thick. The King said, "I am sure that this is all of the knowledge in the world, but no one is going to read all of this! You will need to condense it."

So, the scholars went back to work, and returned to the King with the revised edition, which were only four books. The King said, "Well, that's better, but it is still too long."

The scholars went away to condense some more, each time being told that it had to be shortened. They had come back with a book, then a chapter, then a page, then a paragraph, and finally, a sentence. The King read the sentence, and exclaimed, "That is it; that is truly the wisdom of the ages! If everyone would learn this wisdom and take it to heart, the world will be perfect!"

The sentence simply said. "There ain't no free lunch."

The American Dream was build on that premise; that you could get everything you wanted if you would work hard, work smart, and live within your means. Work is one of the lost arts in America. Our parents and grandparents have worked hard to make life easier for their children and grandchildren. The question is: did they do us any favors?

The reality is that the only place that success comes before work is in the dictionary. The cases that I have worked on showed the unfortunate tendency for Americans to try to make money the easy way rather than the honest way. I spoke to the District Attorney's office in one case, and the investigator said that he once worked in vice, and thought he had seen it all. When he started working in the real estate fraud division, he could not believe what people would do to other people, just for the sake of money.

Thomas Jefferson once said, "Money, and not morality, is the principle of commercial nations." What foresight he had, yet in early 2008, our government could not see 2 years ahead to where we were going.

Of course, there is a very simple reason why they could not find the time to address the issues that were staring in the face of our nation's and the world's economy. It was an election year, and both parties were going through the primaries to determine who would be running for president, and which party could get control of the government.

By the time the dust had settled in November, 2008, the avalanche had started and the tokens to stimulate the economy were simply not enough. Everyone in the country received a $600 stimulus check in order to kick start the economy. When you are unemployed with a $3,500 per month mortgage, that money doesn't go too far. When your neighbor loses his job, the country is in a recession. When you lose YOUR job, the country is in a depression.

How could the little guy stand up for himself against the banks, servicers, investors, and the government? According to J.P. Morgan, "I don't want a lawyer to tell me what I cannot do; I hire him to tell me how to do what I want to do." In the banking panics of 1906, J. P. Morgan took over banks that were on the verge of failure. Over the past 2 years, J.P. Morgan – Chase has taken over numerous banks on the verge of failure, including a sweet deal with the help of the FDIC when Chase acquired Washington Mutual Bank, one of the biggest bank failures in history. Part of that sweet deal was paid for by taxpayers.

I said earlier that I would tell you why I believe the government acted as they did in bailing out the banks, rather than directing their actions to determining exactly what caused the problem and a realistic way of addressing the problem.

First, the government likes to do things big ... $800 billion infusion to the economy (banking system) to shore things up. While it may have worked in the past, the disasters at a personal level overshadowed the specter of that big number. The people who had been duped by the mortgage products developed by Wall Street and the Banks felt nothing for those entities, and wondered when the government would bail them out. That, of course, never happened.

Second, the banks were low on money. How could the possibly maintain the high level of campaign contributions to the politicians and the political parties without a treasure trove of cash? The word "Politics" come from two Latin words: Poly, meaning many, and tics, meaning voracious blood suckers.

Finally, we are represented by people who have one overriding thing on their minds, to get re-elected. Once they get a taste of power, any trace of common sense that they had goes out the window. I am convinced that when someone gets elected to public office, prior to being sworn in, he is taken to the hospital where he or she has "Common Sense Bypass" surgery, and it is replaces by an insatiable desire to be re-elected.

President Abraham Lincoln said that a house divided among itself cannot long stand. Our country has been polarized for many years, but especially since the Viet Nam war. We have the ultra liberals and the ultra conservatives, both taking verbal pot shots at the other. We must endure the Rush Limbaugh's on one side and the Al Sharpton's on the other. More socialism versus more conservatism. What we see, however, is when a more liberal party is in control of the government, they try to pull the country to the left, and the conservatives move closer to the center. Those in the center get fed up with the liberal attitudes, and start voting for the conservative party which has become more centrist. But then, the conservative party tries to move the country to the right, and the liberals start to move more to the center. Back and forth it goes, and no one has figured out that if you just do what is right for the majority of the people all of the time, rather than the special interest groups that contribute to them (and that happens with both sides), that party could stay in power forever.

Who would like to join me in starting the "Common Sense Party?"

The idea of job creation is good, but shouldn't we be working on the creation of permanent jobs, rather than interim jobs? Public-work projects to work on the infrastructure that has been ignored for years is fine, but what happens when those are completed?

Many people say that capitalism is bad, which of course is not true. Greedy and unregulated capitalism can be bad. Let's take a simple example of how capitalism is supposed to work. If you wanted to have a breakfast of Bacon, eggs, coffee and orange juice in the morning, how would you do it without capitalism? You could either raise chickens and pigs, and grow oranges and coffee beans, or, you would need to track down someone else who does so you could buy those items from them. If you live in Iowa, will you have time to run down to Florida and Brazil to get the oranges and coffee?

Capitalism is taking your own money, or bringing it together from others, to form a business that sells those things to the consumer. These do not happen for free, and whoever is taking the risk of bringing those items together for people to buy, hoping that they will do so, has the right to make a profit. The consumer, through competition and the law of supply and demand, will generally create a fair market price for the commodity.

Let's take it down one more notch. A 10 year old child buys an old, beat up bicycle for $2 from a friend. The child cleans the bike, puts new tires on it, paints it and makes sure it is shiny and like new. He invested $4 of parts and paint in order to make the bicycle like new, and sells it for $10. Is a 10 year old kid entitled to a profit of $4? The answer is, of course. The world now has a shiny bicycle instead of a beat up eyesore.

The problem that we have experienced with the mortgage issues and drop in the economy did not come from capitalism, it came from unregulated capitalism. Just as unregulated communism and socialism can be bad, unregulated capitalism can be bad, too. The OTC derivatives were not a physical product that would be consumed, but an investment gamble in which the only definite winners would be the ones who developed the "product."

I believe that real estate will come back and be a viable investment hedge against inflation. However, it is also my belief, and I think should be the demand by every American, that our elected representative start working in the best interest of the country and the people, rather than the deep pockets of the political contributors. Unfortunately, our Supreme Court, in an unwise decision, stated that a corporation, and artificial "person" developed by laws, has the right of free speech and the right to use its money to promote specific candidates.

We should demand that management and labor begin working together to maintain the strength of the companies that they represent. A corporation is like a ship, and when the ship sinks, everyone loses. Management needs workers, and workers need the company to survive in order to have a job.

We need to enforce education on the youth of America, rather than just provide it for free. Education is your ticket to freedom, and it is the one thing that no one can ever take away from you. Kids tend to get caught up in the possibility of making millions of dollars in football, baseball or basketball, and many parents, especially in the more depressed areas of our country, encourage that belief. The reality is that a kid is more likely to be successful as a doctor, attorney or some other profession than he is in sports.

I tell kids that Steve Young, one of the best quarterbacks in the past 30 years, knew that athletics could be fleeting, and that one injury could end his career. That is why he finished his education and continued on to law school. He didn't need it, but he knew that there were no guarantees.

Our country must invest in itself with some tax incentives for companies to maintain operations in the United States, or perhaps some tax penalties for taking the operations to other countries. We must invest in alternative forms of energy, such as solar and wind, as well as other sources of fuel other than from oil. We are making ethanol form corn products, but that could also cause a long term food shortage. It is also a fact that Brazil has learned that sugar actually produces better ethanol at a lower cost than that made from corn. Why are we not growing sugar cane in this country?

We are in a global economy, and what happens here will have an effect on every corner of the planet. What happens in other countries can have an effect on America, too. The main difference between the United States and many other countries is that we have forgotten the meaning of work. As I said in the beginning, the American Dream has become, "Get Rich Quick, at any cost." We as individuals and a nation must return to the idea of get rich slowly by initiative, hard work and frugality.

In other words, "There Ain't No Free Lunch!"

Appendix A

This chart is the numbers used for the calculations of projected median prices of homes in California. The following is an explanation of each column, and its relationship to the overall chart and projection formula.

Year – The year for which the statistics pertain.

California Population - The actual population for the year in question.

Increase - The increase in actual population over the previous year.

% Increase – The Percentage of increase of population over the previous year.

1.4% of Population Increase – The actual percentage increase multiplied by 1.4, and the number added to the rate of Inflation in the formula.

Inflation – The actual rate of inflation for the year in question.

Factor – The number used in the formula multiplied by the previous year's "Projected Median Price"

Cal. Median Price – The previous year's Projected Median Price.

Increase – The projected increase of the median price over the last year's projected median price.

Projected Med. Price – The new projected median price of California homes.

Actual Median Price – The actual Median Price for homes that year.

Percent Over/Under – The percentage that the actual median price was over or under the projected median price.

Prime Rate – The average prime rate for the year in question.

The formula as used in this chart projects the median price starting with 1968 through 2009, with no regard to what the actual median price was for a given year.

Year	California Population	Increase	Pop. % Increase	1.4 x Pop. Increase	Inflation	Factor	Starting Median Home Price	Cal. Median Price Increase	Projected Med. Price	Actual Median Price	Percent Over/Under	Prime Rate
1968	19,432,000						23,210.00			23,210.00	N/A	6.50
1969	19,745,000	313,000	1.59	2.22	5.46	7.68	23,210.00	1,782.36	24,992.36	24,230.00	-3.15%	8.00
1970	20,039,000	294,000	1.47	2.20	5.84	8.04	24,230.00	1,948.26	26,178.26	24,640.00	-6.24%	7.00
1971	20,346,000	307,000	1.51	2.26	4.30	6.56	24,640.00	1,617.21	26,257.21	26,880.00	2.32%	5.75
1972	20,585,000	239,000	1.16	1.74	3.27	5.01	26,880.00	1,347.11	28,227.11	28,810.00	2.02%	5.25
1973	20,869,000	284,000	1.36	2.04	6.16	8.20	28,810.00	2,362.80	31,172.80	31,460.00	0.91%	8.25
1974	21,174,000	305,000	1.44	2.16	11.03	13.19	31,460.00	4,149.78	35,609.78	34,610.00	-2.89%	10.25
1975	21,538,000	364,000	1.69	2.54	9.20	11.74	34,610.00	4,061.50	38,671.50	41,600.00	7.04%	8.25
1976	21,936,000	398,000	1.81	2.72	5.75	8.47	41,600.00	3,524.17	45,124.17	48,630.00	7.21%	6.75
1977	22,352,000	416,000	1.86	2.79	6.50	9.29	48,630.00	4,518.55	53,148.55	62,290.00	14.69%	7.25
1978	22,836,000	484,000	2.12	3.18	7.62	10.80	62,290.00	6,726.82	69,016.82	70,890.00	2.64%	9.25
1979	23,257,000	421,000	1.81	2.72	11.22	13.94	70,890.00	9,878.74	80,768.74	84,150.00	4.02%	13.75
1980	23,782,000	525,000	2.21	3.31	13.58	16.89	84,150.00	14,214.05	98,364.05	99,550.00	1.19%	15.75
1981	24,278,000	496,000	2.04	3.06	10.35	13.41	99,550.00	13,354.14	112,904.14	107,710.00	-4.82%	18.25
1982	24,805,000	527,000	2.12	3.19	6.16	9.35	107,710.00	10,067.50	117,777.50	111,800.00	-5.35%	14.50
1983	25,337,000	532,000	2.10	3.15	3.22	6.37	111,800.00	7,121.15	118,921.15	114,370.00	-3.98%	10.75
1984	25,816,000	479,000	1.86	2.78	4.30	7.08	114,370.00	8,101.01	122,471.01	114,260.00	-7.19%	12.50
1985	26,403,000	587,000	2.22	3.33	3.55	6.88	114,260.00	7,866.63	122,126.63	119,860.00	-1.89%	10.00
1986	27,052,000	649,000	2.40	3.60	1.91	5.51	119,860.00	6,602.64	126,462.64	133,640.00	5.37%	8.25
1987	27,717,000	665,000	2.40	3.60	3.66	7.26	133,640.00	9,700.76	143,340.76	142,060.00	-0.90%	7.50
1988	28,393,000	676,000	2.38	3.57	4.08	7.65	142,060.00	10,869.44	152,929.44	168,200.00	9.08%	9.50
1989	29,142,000	749,000	2.57	3.86	4.83	8.69	168,200.00	14,608.61	182,808.61	196,120.00	6.79%	9.75
1990	29,828,000	686,000	2.30	3.45	5.39	8.84	196,120.00	17,336.57	213,456.57	193,770.00	-10.16%	11.00
1991	30,458,000	630,000	2.07	3.10	4.25	7.35	193,770.00	14,247.20	208,017.20	200,660.00	-3.67%	8.50
1992	30,987,000	529,000	1.71	2.56	3.03	5.59	200,660.00	11,218.40	211,878.40	197,030.00	-7.54%	6.00
1993	31,314,000	327,000	1.04	1.57	2.96	4.53	197,030.00	8,918.35	205,948.35	188,240.00	-9.41%	6.00
1994	31,523,000	209,000	0.66	0.99	2.61	3.60	188,240.00	6,785.13	195,025.13	185,010.00	-5.41%	7.50
1995	31,711,000	188,000	0.59	0.89	2.81	3.70	185,010.00	6,844.04	191,854.04	178,160.00	-7.69%	8.50
1996	31,962,000	251,000	0.79	1.18	2.93	4.11	178,160.00	7,318.74	185,478.74	177,270.00	-4.63%	8.25
1997	32,452,000	490,000	1.51	2.26	2.34	4.60	177,270.00	8,163.08	185,433.08	186,490.00	0.57%	8.50
1998	32,862,000	410,000	1.25	1.87	1.55	3.42	186,490.00	6,380.69	192,870.69	200,100.00	3.61%	8.00
1999	33,417,000	555,000	1.66	2.49	2.19	4.68	200,100.00	9,367.18	209,467.18	217,510.00	3.70%	8.00
2000	34,099,000	682,000	2.00	3.00	3.38	6.38	217,510.00	13,877.33	231,387.33	241,350.00	4.13%	9.25
2001	34,784,000	685,000	1.97	2.95	2.83	5.78	241,350.00	13,959.55	255,309.55	262,350.00	2.68%	6.75
2002	35,393,000	609,000	1.72	2.58	1.59	4.17	262,350.00	10,942.67	273,292.67	316,130.00	13.55%	4.25
2003	35,990,000	597,000	1.66	2.49	2.27	4.76	316,130.00	15,042.07	331,172.07	371,520.00	10.86%	4.00
2004	35,894,000	(96,000)	-0.27	-0.40	2.68	2.28	371,520.00	8,466.27	379,986.27	450,990.00	15.74%	4.75
2005	36,458,000	564,000	1.55	2.32	3.39	5.71	450,990.00	25,753.69	476,743.69	524,020.00	9.02%	6.25
2006	37,444,000	986,000	2.63	3.95	3.24	7.19	524,020.00	37,676.51	561,696.51	556,240.00	-0.98%	7.75
2007	37,559,440	115,440	0.31	0.46	2.85	3.31	556,240.00	18,417.27	574,657.27	558,100.00	-2.97%	8.25
2008	38,049,000	489,560	1.29	1.93	3.85	5.78	558,100.00	32,258.10	590,358.10	346,750.00	-70.25%	5.00
2009	38,293,000	244,000	0.64	0.96	-0.94	0.02	346,750.00	54.75	346,804.75	306,820.00	-13.03%	3.25

134

Appendix B

This chart is the numbers used for the calculations of projected median prices of homes in California based upon the actual median price for the previous year. The following is an explanation of each column, and its relationship to the overall chart and projection formula.

Year – The year for which the statistics pertain.

California Population - The actual population for the year in question.

Increase - The increase in actual population over the previous year.

% Increase – The Percentage of increase of population over the previous year.

1.4% of Population Increase – The actual percentage increase multiplied by 1.4, and the number added to the rate of Inflation in the formula.

Inflation – The actual rate of inflation for the year in question.

Factor – The number used in the formula multiplied by the previous year's "Actual Median Price"

Cal. Median Price – The previous year's Projected Median Price.

Increase – The projected increase of the median price over the last year's Actual median price.

Projected Med. Price – The new projected median price of California homes.

Actual Median Price – The actual Median Price for homes that year.

Percent Over/Under – The percentage that the actual median price was over or under the projected median price.

Prime Rate – The average prime rate for the year in question.

The formula as used in this chart projects the median price starting with 1968, and then using the formula against the actual median price for each year.

Year	California Population	Increase	% Increase	1.4% of Pop. Increase	Inflation	Factor	Cal Median Price	Increase	Projected Med. Price	Actual Median Price	Percent Over/Under	Prime Rate
1968	19,432,000	257,000	1.34	1.88	4.27	6.15	23,575.26	1,449.03	25,024.29	23,210.00	-7.82%	6.50
1969	19,745,000	313,000	1.61	2.26	5.46	7.72	25,024.29	1,930.63	26,954.92	24,230.00	-11.25%	8.00
1970	20,039,000	294,000	1.49	2.08	5.84	7.92	26,954.92	2,136.06	29,090.99	24,640.00	-18.06%	7.00
1971	20,346,000	307,000	1.53	2.14	4.30	6.44	29,090.99	1,874.86	30,965.85	26,880.00	-15.20%	5.75
1972	20,585,000	239,000	1.17	1.64	3.27	4.91	30,965.85	1,521.83	32,487.68	28,810.00	-12.77%	5.25
1973	20,869,000	284,000	1.38	1.93	6.16	8.09	32,487.68	2,628.74	35,116.42	31,460.00	-11.62%	8.25
1974	21,174,000	305,000	1.46	2.05	11.03	13.08	35,116.42	4,591.86	39,708.28	34,610.00	-14.73%	10.25
1975	21,538,000	364,000	1.72	2.41	9.20	11.61	39,708.28	4,608.83	44,317.11	41,600.00	-6.53%	8.25
1976	21,936,000	398,000	1.85	2.59	5.75	8.34	44,317.11	3,694.74	48,011.86	48,630.00	1.27%	6.75
1977	22,352,000	416,000	1.90	2.65	6.50	9.15	48,011.86	4,395.48	52,407.34	62,290.00	15.87%	7.25
1978	22,836,000	484,000	2.17	3.03	7.62	10.65	52,407.34	5,582.17	57,989.50	70,890.00	18.20%	9.25
1979	23,257,000	421,000	1.84	2.58	11.22	13.80	57,989.50	8,003.14	65,992.64	84,150.00	21.58%	13.75
1980	23,782,000	525,000	2.26	3.16	13.58	16.74	65,992.64	11,047.39	77,040.04	99,550.00	22.61%	15.75
1981	24,278,000	496,000	2.09	2.92	10.35	13.27	77,040.04	10,223.10	87,263.14	107,710.00	18.98%	18.25
1982	24,805,000	527,000	2.17	3.04	6.16	9.20	87,263.14	8,027.31	95,290.44	111,800.00	14.77%	14.50
1983	25,337,000	532,000	2.14	3.00	3.22	6.22	95,290.44	5,929.56	101,220.01	114,370.00	11.50%	10.75
1984	25,816,000	479,000	1.89	2.65	4.30	6.95	101,220.01	7,031.47	108,251.48	114,260.00	5.26%	12.50
1985	26,403,000	587,000	2.27	3.18	3.55	6.73	108,251.48	7,288.89	115,540.37	119,860.00	3.60%	10.00
1986	27,052,000	649,000	2.46	3.44	1.91	5.35	115,540.37	6,182.88	121,723.26	133,640.00	8.92%	8.25
1987	27,717,000	665,000	2.46	3.44	3.66	7.10	121,723.26	8,644.20	130,367.46	142,060.00	8.23%	9.50
1988	28,393,000	676,000	2.44	3.41	4.08	7.49	130,367.46	9,770.40	140,137.86	168,200.00	16.68%	9.75
1989	29,142,000	749,000	2.64	3.69	4.83	8.52	140,137.86	11,944.18	152,082.04	196,120.00	22.45%	11.00
1990	29,828,000	686,000	2.35	3.30	5.39	8.69	152,082.04	13,209.22	165,291.26	193,770.00	14.70%	10.00
1991	30,458,000	630,000	2.11	2.96	4.25	7.21	165,291.26	11,912.46	177,203.72	200,660.00	11.69%	8.50
1992	30,987,000	529,000	1.74	2.43	3.03	5.46	177,203.72	9,678.06	186,881.78	197,030.00	5.15%	6.00
1993	31,314,000	327,000	1.06	1.48	2.96	4.44	186,881.78	8,292.68	195,174.46	188,240.00	-3.68%	6.00
1994	31,523,000	209,000	0.67	0.93	2.61	3.54	195,174.46	6,917.78	202,092.24	185,010.00	-9.23%	7.50
1995	31,711,000	188,000	0.60	0.83	2.81	3.64	202,092.24	7,366.15	209,458.39	178,160.00	-17.57%	8.50
1996	31,962,000	251,000	0.79	1.11	2.93	4.04	209,458.39	8,458.21	217,916.60	177,270.00	-22.93%	8.25
1997	32,452,000	490,000	1.53	2.15	2.34	4.49	217,916.60	9,776.39	227,692.99	186,490.00	-22.09%	8.50
1998	32,862,000	410,000	1.26	1.77	1.55	3.32	227,692.99	7,556.60	235,249.59	200,100.00	-17.57%	8.25
1999	33,417,000	555,000	1.69	2.36	2.19	4.55	235,249.59	10,714.28	245,963.87	217,510.00	-13.08%	8.00
2000	34,099,000	682,000	2.04	2.86	3.38	6.24	245,963.87	15,341.33	261,305.20	241,350.00	-8.27%	9.25
2001	34,784,000	685,000	2.01	2.81	2.83	5.64	261,305.20	14,743.88	276,049.08	262,350.00	-5.22%	6.75
2002	35,393,000	609,000	1.75	2.45	1.59	4.04	276,049.08	11,155.49	287,204.58	316,130.00	9.15%	4.25
2003	35,990,000	597,000	1.69	2.36	2.27	4.63	287,204.58	13,301.83	300,506.41	371,520.00	19.11%	4.00
2004	35,894,000	(96,000)	-0.27	-0.37	2.68	4.75	300,506.41	14,272.44	314,778.85	450,990.00	30.20%	4.25
2005	36,458,000	564,000	1.57	2.20	3.39	5.15	314,778.85	16,221.56	331,000.42	524,020.00	36.83%	6.25
2006	37,444,000	986,000	2.70	3.79	3.24	4.99	331,000.42	16,513.47	347,513.89	556,240.00	37.52%	8.00
2007	37,559,440	115,440	0.31	0.43	2.85	4.60	347,513.89	15,982.02	363,495.91	558,100.00	34.87%	7.75
2008	38,049,000	489,560	1.30	1.82	3.85	5.60	363,495.91	20,351.99	383,847.90	346,750.00	-10.70%	5.00
2009	38,293,000	244,000	0.64	0.90	-0.94	0.81	383,847.90	3,105.17	386,953.07	306,820.00	-26.12%	3.25

137

Appendix C –

These are the same graphs used in Chapter 10, but using the numbers from Appendix B instead of Appendix A, and applying the formula to the actual previous year's median price instead of the projected previous year's median price.

1968 through 1976

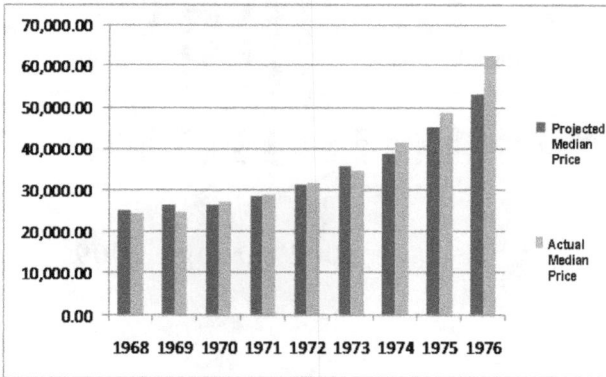

1977 through 1988

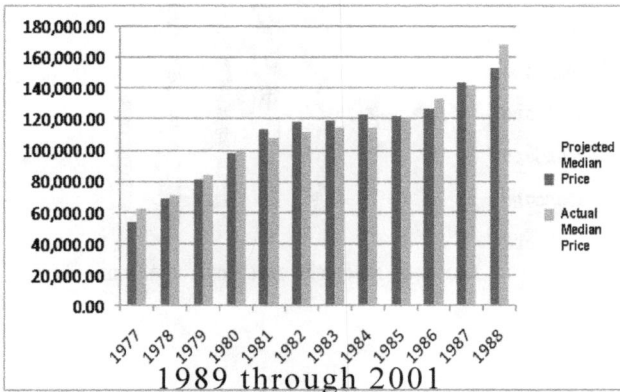

1989 through 2001

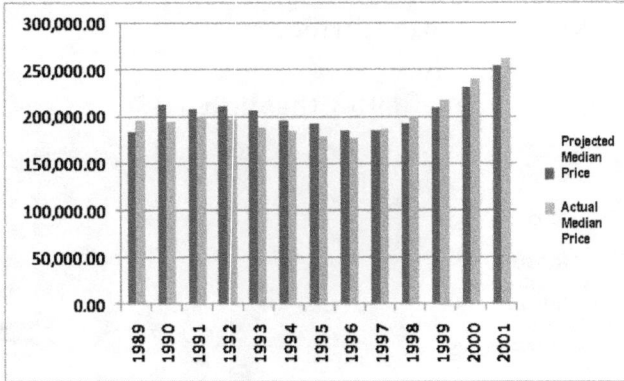

2002 through 2009

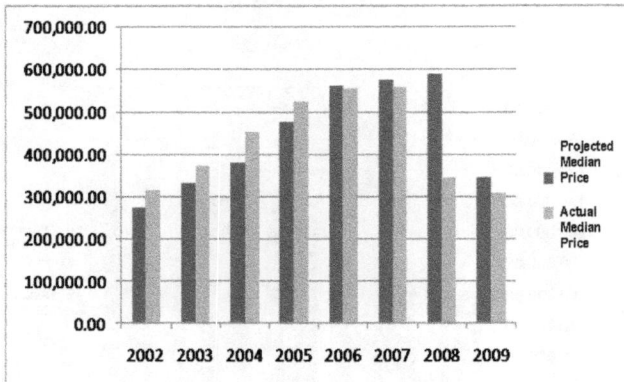